SO YOU WANT TO GO TO GRADUATE SCHOOL?

SO YOU WANT TO GO TO GRADUATE SCHOOL?

WHAT YOU NEED TO KNOW ABOUT GRADUATE SCHOOL, BUT MAY NOT HAVE KNOWN YOU NEEDED TO ASK

Kenneth L. Poff
Emeritus Professor of Horticulture
and Botany and of Plant Pathology
Michigan State University

and

William R. Gordon
Master Teacher of Biology
Howard University

With a Preface by
Karen L. Klomparens
Graduate School Dean
Michigan State University

Illustrated by Jess Herrington

Published in the United States by Ziibi Press. <ziibi.org>

ISBN: **978-0-9830894-0-7**

First Printing: November, 2010
Second Printing: January, 2011
Third Printing: April, 2011

cknowledgements

We gratefully acknowledge and thank colleagues and students for the hundreds of extremely thoughtful and helpful comments on drafts of this book. We firmly believe that the book has been immeasurably improved by this process. Others have been able to see areas for improvement that we were unable to see ourselves.

The two of us have succeeded through the help of many who provided us with guidance along our paths. Notable among these have been Dr. William R. Tenney, Dr. Virgil Greene Lilly, Karl Norris, Professor Dr. Wolfgang Haupt, Dr. Gaye Burpee, and Dr. James H. M. Henderson. For these mentors, we are truly thankful.

We gratefully thank the many students from whom we have learned so much.

Daryl Davis, Dr. Radomir Konjevic and Dr. George Rowan have provided us with extraordinary examples of the power of communication across cultural boundaries.

We have sincerely appreciated the editorial assistance of Dr. Phil Bellfy, editor and publisher of the Ziibi Press.

In our personal lives we are thankful for the support of Holly Schaeffer, Rebecca Hehl, and Georgia Ann Gordon.

Finally, we have become brothers in spite of the process of writing together.

*T*able of Contents

Preface

Foreword
A. To the student
B. About the authors

A. Your application.
B. The selection process.
C. The interview.
D. Follow-up after the interview.

A. Fellowships.
B. Teaching assistantships.
C. Research assistantships.
D. Obtain your own funding.

A. Time line for a course work master's program.
B. Time line for a research master's program.
C. Time line for a PhD program.

Preface

Behind every successful graduate student, especially a Ph.D. student, is a mentor, or better yet, multiple mentors or coaches. What do these mentors or coaches do to help ensure student success? They tell you the truth. They tell you the truth in answer to your questions. And, they tell you the truth about questions you didn't even know to ask. That truth may be uncomfortable. It may be embarrassing. It may fill you with pride or happiness. It may feel like criticism. And, sometimes, you won't agree with it and perhaps shouldn't. But if you have a mentor or coach, or multiple mentors or coaches who you can trust, that truthful advice is priceless.

Dr. Poff and Dr. Gordon provide exactly that truthful advice in *So You Want to go to Graduate School?* Even if you don't know them personally, they can act as your mentors/coaches through the pages of this book. At its core, this book provides "insider" information that will help you successfully navigate the admission process, find financial support, choose an advisor and guidance committee members, and pursue courses and research. They demystify comprehensive exams, departmental politics, and the essentials of those all-important life skills that are needed to be considered a "professional". While this may seem daunting, you can succeed!

This information in this book and Dr. Poff and Dr. Gordon's insights are what good faculty mentors share with their students or if not shared, students may stumble on these items of wisdom by accident, through friends, or by making mistakes. You don't need to stumble along! The key advice is here for you to read, understand, and try.

The underlying assumption is <u>not</u> that graduate study is too complex to explain or that some students deserve the information and advice and other don't. Graduate students, postdoctoral trainees, and especially faculty are passionately focused on the knowledge in the discipline, on synthesizing that knowledge, generating new knowledge, and disseminating that new knowledge through teaching, publications, and professional publications. The ideas, the discussions (and arguments), and research are the main attractions. Sometimes faculty members just don't remember to give students the "insider" advice, because it is not the research and ideas that they love. But, this information is <u>vitally</u> important!

There are politics in every single organization. No exceptions. Your experience in graduate school, plus the advice in the book, will teach you how to watch for and navigate through the politics anywhere you are. *So You Want to go to Graduate School?* is your guide to the myths, lore, unwritten rules, and implicit expectations in graduate school.

I've known Ken Poff and Bill Gordon for more than two decades. I've watched them successfully coach and mentor students. In this book they tell the truth in a plain and straightforward way. Let them help you succeed.

Read this book! Ask questions of your undergraduate and graduate faculty mentors and coaches. You can be successful in graduate school, and when you are, I hope you'll "pay it forward" and be an effective coach or mentor for the next generation of graduate students by sharing the advice from this book.

Good luck! I wish you every success.

Karen L Klomparens
Dean of the Graduate School, Michigan State University, 2010

Foreword

One of the authors (KLP) has participated in a number of workshops for minority students considering graduate school. It has become evident during those workshops and in discussions afterward that many, if not most, students have much of the explicit information that is contained in handbooks, catalogs, *etc*, but lack implicit or "insider" information about the nature of graduate school.

In fact, in most cases, the lack of information is so extensive that the student does not even know what questions to formulate (hence, the title of this book). Many of the undergraduates who should be seriously considering graduate school have no opportunities to learn about this next potential step in their education.

In forty years of dealing with students in a number of universities, the authors observed that most students who are accepted into graduate school and who subsequently do not succeed seldom leave because of an inability to handle the intellectual challenges placed on them in graduate school.

The lack of success for many of the students who leave graduate school without a degree can be attributed either to their floundering in the politics in their institution, or their inability to adapt sufficiently rapidly from dependence on the set of skills that ensured their success as an undergraduate student to development of a set of skills that will ensure their success as a graduate student. This is often referred to as a lack of "socialization."

This book is written in an attempt to share and teach those political and social skills that are necessary for success in graduate school. It is the hope of the authors that this will permit an increased number of previously marginalized students to successfully pursue advanced degrees.

To the student:
As you read through this book, you will find many suggestions that are intended to assist you in the transition into and through graduate school. Many of the suggestions come from the authors' experiences in the biological sciences. You have every right to reject any of the suggestions that seem distasteful to you for whatever reason. These suggestions are designed to assist you on your own personal journey of intellectual growth. They have been carefully considered to provide you with the knowledge base with which you can make your own decisions. Every life is about decisions, and it is our hope that you will feel empowered by having the information in this book. Make your decisions the best ones possible.

About the authors:

Ken Poff was the first person in his extended family to attend and graduate from college. He successfully completed a master's degree and PhD, and went on to teach in several universities. He is currently Emeritus Professor of Horticulture and of Plant Biology at Michigan State University. The courses he has taught have included "Introductory Plant Physiology" and "Environmental Plant Physiology" at the undergraduate level, and "Environmental Plant Physiology" at the graduate level.

In addition, during his last fifteen years at MSU, he worked to increase minority representation in the plant sciences and this has led to a second interest as an academician in "the culture of science." In this context, he periodically has taught a graduate course on "Mentoring and Teaching in a Culturally Diverse Environment," and participated in an Honor's course on "Critical Incident Analysis." He also teaches workshops and lectures for faculty, undergraduate and graduate students on "Gender and Equity," and "The Mentor-student Relationship."

Ken chaired the graduate affairs committee for the Plant Research Laboratory at MSU for over five years, and has served on approximately 100 advisory committees for graduate students in Botany and Plant Pathology, Crop and Soil Sciences, Forestry and Horticulture. In addition, he served for two years as Interim Associate Dean for Diversity and Pluralism in the College of Agriculture and Natural Resources.

William Gordon has served as the Biology Director of the Research Experiences for Undergraduates Program at the National Science Foundation. He is currently a member of the faculty of the Biology Department at Howard University in Washington, D.C. He was born and reared in Richmond, Virginia.

After earning the B.S. degree in Biology at Tuskegee University, he worked as an Epidemiologist for the Communicable Disease Center of the U. S. Department of Health, Education and Welfare in New York City. Upon completion of a Master of Science degree at Tuskegee University, he pursued and completed a PhD degree in Plant Physiology and Biochemistry at the University of Minnesota-Twin Cities. Following seventeen months as a Research Associate at the Brookhaven National Laboratory, he joined the faculty of the Department of Botany and Microbiology at Howard University.

During Bill's 35-year tenure at Howard University, he has taught thirteen different graduate and undergraduate courses and has mentored fourteen graduate students, five of whom received the Master of Science degree under his guidance. One of his master's students continued her studies to earn the PhD degree in Plant Physiology at the University of California at Berkeley. Gordon has served as the Faculty Adviser for the Howard University Chapter of the Beta Kappa Chi National Scientific Honor Society since 1983.

In collaboration with Ken Poff, Bill established the Minority Researchers in Plant Sciences Program at Michigan State University. He has devoted much of his career to seeking avenues to enhance opportunities for minorities and members of other under-represented groups to pursue research careers in the biological and agricultural sciences. He currently serves as the Alliance Coordinator for the National Science Foundation-funded Washington Baltimore Hampton Roads-Louis Stokes Alliance for Minority Participation Program (WBHR-LSAMP) at Howard University.

What is Graduate School?

You are considering continuing your education beyond the bachelor's degree. Perhaps one of your undergraduate faculty suggested that you should consider graduate school; perhaps you've heard that the opportunities are greater if you have a graduate degree; or perhaps you know that a master's or Ph.D. degree is necessary for entry into your profession of choice. For whatever reason, you are now considering graduate school. If you are like the majority of students, you really don't know exactly what graduate school is. You've never heard a family member or

1

friend talk about their experiences in graduate school. In fact, your undergraduate professors may be the only people you know who have been to graduate school, and your professors may not have been the type to informally ask questions like: "So, what's graduate school like?" Read on; by the time you've read through this book, you should have a better idea of what graduate school is, how it is different from undergraduate school, and what is necessary to succeed in graduate school.

First, although a graduate degree may typically be required for some careers, such as university professor, graduate school is not necessarily preparation for a particular career. If the graduate degree is preparation for a career in a particular area, such as engineering, it is usually referred to as a professional graduate degree. Some doctoral degrees may prepare one for a particular profession such as the MD or DO for the medical profession. Others are more general.

For example, the Ph.D. is designed to prepare one to do research in a specific area called a discipline such as history or chemistry. This booklet is designed particularly for the student considering a graduate, non-professional degree. This degree will be either a master's degree or Ph.D. degree (doctor of philosophy).

With a graduate degree, your lifetime earnings will probably be higher than without that degree. You may need the advanced degree as entry into a particular career such as university professor. You may want the degree so that in your chosen research career, you will be designing the research project and not working in a technical capacity in the research program designed by someone else. All of these may well apply. However there is one characteristic that can generally be applied to the person seeking a

2

master's or Ph.D. degree, and that is a *love of knowledge, and a love of the pursuit of knowledge.*

If you have found yourself with an incredible appetite for knowledge; if the typical undergraduate course leaves you with more unanswered questions than answers; if you find yourself constantly wanting to go beyond the usual explanations, then you should definitely go to graduate school and seek an advanced degree.
However, be aware that the set of experiences in graduate school will likely not satisfy your hunger. More probably, as you learn more, the horizon of the unknown will continue to expand. However, the graduate experience is designed to acquaint you with the methods for acquiring and disseminating knowledge in your chosen field.

For further information, see Kidwell, C. S., and J. B. LaPidus. *Graduate School and you. A guide for prospective graduate students.* Council of Graduate Schools, Washington, D.C. 1989.

What Does the Application Process for Graduate School Look Like?

From the outside, the application process to get accepted into graduate school can look like a game of chance. However, this is actually a well-defined process. In this section, we will go through the process step by step. This section certainly won't guarantee your acceptance, but it should clarify the process and the critical steps.

Your application.
Once your application is complete, it will be evaluated by a person

or committee in your chosen department. The application itself consists of three main components: your transcript and grade point average, your Graduate Record Examination scores (GRE's) or your scores on some other standardized test, and your letters of reference. In addition, there are two additional important pieces: your cover letter and your statement of purpose. Unfortunately, we cannot tell you that your entire file will be examined. Although your file *should* be looked at in its entirety, many departments will use threshold scores for the two numerical scores: your grade point average, and your Graduate Record Examination scores. Unfortunately these departments will **only** pay attention to your letters of reference if the two numerical scores exceed the department's threshold. If your two numerical scores do exceed the department's threshold values, then the letters and statement of purpose will become extremely important. This statement of purpose is used to screen for a best fit to a particular faculty interest.

One of the best predictors for success in graduate school, particularly in a doctoral program, is your past success in a research environment. Although there is no formal place for this item to be displayed on your application, there are several places for you to highlight such an experience. Have you worked in a research capacity with anyone in your undergraduate experience? This could be as an intern in a summer program; this could be as a volunteer working with one of your professors. If you have the time left before applying for graduate school, try to find a research experience. How do you highlight this experience? Ask for a letter of reference from the person with whom you have worked. In the statement of purpose in your application, mention your research experiences. Later, in the interview, when you're asked about any research experiences, be prepared to discuss what you did, how you did it, what its significance was, and where that research would appropriately lead next.

Your transcript and grade point average.
The higher your grade point average (GPA) for your undergraduate
education, the better is your chance of acceptance into a good
graduate program. In general, a GPA of 3.5 or greater out of 4.0
will guarantee that your file will be read closely. With a GPA
below 3.0 out of 4.0, you will have difficulties gaining acceptance
into a major institution. As is evident to any thoughtful person, the
GPA does not tell the entire story of the undergraduate
performance. Much depends on the institution, the courses taken,
and the other activities combined with the course of studies.
However, it is likely that the acceptance committee will look very
carefully at the GPA and the institution from which the transcript
has come, and then look on the transcript for your grades in those
courses considered to be very important for your field. In general,
to maximize the probabilities of acceptance, keep your
undergraduate grades up but don't avoid the challenging courses.
If your GPA improved during your last two years as an
undergraduate, point that out in your application (probably in your
cover letter).

Apply to more than one institution at the same time. If your
application is declined by your institution of choice because of
your low GPA, go to the next institution on your list. In other
words, do not place all of your eggs in the same basket. If
accepted, you have the opportunity to demonstrate that the earlier
GPA was anomalous and does not adequately represent your
potential.

Your Graduate Record Examination scores:
Most departments, particularly in the sciences and engineering,
require Graduate Record Examination (GRE) scores for admission
to graduate school, especially for doctoral programs. It is unlikely
that you will be considered for financial assistance without the
GRE scores. This is a nationally administered, standardized test

that purports to test the enhancement of your knowledge and skills since high school.

There are four components to the examination: verbal, quantitative, analytical, and advanced. The first three of these are frequently the required components. Many departments have a threshold value for the percentile scores on the GRE, and a low score can mean that your entire file is not considered. Prepare yourself for the GRE with the following steps.

- Visit the testing center at your college or university and avail yourself of any assistance they may offer on preparation for the GRE.
- Find a book on how to prepare for and take the GRE.
- Use the Educational Testing Service GRE test-prep website http://www.ets.org/gre/general/prepare
- Obtain a computer program that will allow you to actually practice for the GRE.
- Rest before the exam, be alert, focus, and do your best.

The paper examination is presently still available although it is being phased out. You can take the paper examination if this is more comfortable for you. It will take you somewhat longer and your score will not be available for about two months. If you choose to take the examination by computer, you can obtain your score immediately. If you have done poorly, begin immediately to prepare yourself for your next try.

The scores on the GREs are historically somewhat lower for certain minority students than for majority students. Don't let this intimidate you. Prepare yourself for the test, practice until you are comfortable with the GRE style of questions, and demonstrate your own abilities.

The GRE is in the process of being revamped. The authors do not anticipate that any changes will alter your need to adequately prepare for the examination.

Your letters of reference:

Except for the fact that some departments use threshold GPA scores and GRE scores, your letters of reference constitute one of the most important parts of your file. Typically you are asked to submit letters from three people who know you sufficiently well to assess your capabilities. This does not mean your friend from next door or a friend of your family. This means three faculty members with whom you have interacted sufficiently closely that they can write an intelligent letter about your preparation for graduate school. This means that you had best not spend your undergraduate career as an anonymous face in the back of your classes.

- Interact with your faculty particularly in your field of interest. If it is at all possible, spend at least one term working for (as a volunteer if necessary) one of your professors. The single most important predictor for success in graduate school in your performance in an "internship," a work situation in your field.
- Carefully consider which faculty to approach for letters. The letter will have less value if the person hardly knows you, has a low opinion of your abilities, or does not him/herself have a graduate degree.
- Approach each professor individually and in person if at all possible. Explain what you wish to do, explain why you believe you will be successful, and ask if they will be willing to write a *positive* letter on your behalf. It is very useful to provide each professor you approach with a short resume. This should summarize your academic career to date. If they decline, or indicate reservations, politely thank them and approach others

9

on your list. If they accept, give them the name and address to whom the letter should be sent, and be willing to talk about the positive attributes that you will take into graduate school.

In other words, be willing to provide them with the descriptors that you honestly believe describe you positively, and that you would like to have included in your letter of reference. Spend time thinking about what will sell you; don't leave that homework for others. You might also ask if you can provide additional information to them by email. That way, the faculty member has an electronic copy of some sentences or paragraphs about you to put in a letter.

The cover letter and statement of purpose:
These are the two pieces of your application that permit you to make your application stand out. The cover letter is the letter to the chairperson of the department or admissions committee indicating that your application is enclosed. The cover letter also is typically read by the admissions committee. Therefore, the cover letter is your opportunity to point out to the admissions committee your major strengths. At the end of this section are two fabricated cover letters. The first says nothing of substance. The second highlights several strengths that the applicant wants the admissions committee to be aware of. Frequently, a good cover letter will result in the entire file being read.

Most graduate school applications forms have a question asking why you want to attend graduate school. This sometimes is asked as two separate statements, a personal statement and a professional statement. Your statement of purpose is your answer to this question. View the statement of purpose as an opportunity to display to an admissions committee who you are and to highlight the reasons why they may want you as a graduate student in their program. Strive to show the reader (the admissions committee) that you are mature (ready for graduate school), and dedicated to advanced professional work in that particular area. While most of the application is somewhat cut and dried, the statement of purpose is the place on the application where you can show your own personality. Having said this, most of the better statements of purpose include four components:

1.   A brief description of who you are as a <u>person</u>.
2.   A short description of who you are as a <u>scholar</u>, with a link between you as a scholar and your application to this particular program.
3.   A paragraph or two in which you help the reader to see you <u>fitting into</u>, <u>learning from</u>, and <u>contributing to</u> their graduate program.
4.   A view of the career you see yourself in following your graduate degree. Remember, the members of the program want to be proud of their graduates. Show them that you have a vision and that they can reasonably expect to be proud of you and your accomplishments.

At the end of this section are four totally fabricated statements of purpose. Read through each and assess it as you think an admissions committee would do. After reading each statement, mentally assign it to one of three stacks labeled "accept," "maybe," and "reject." Try also to put into words **why** you are making that particular assignment. Permit yourself to form a mental image of the applicant. Remember that this is <u>exactly</u> what a member of an admissions committee does. Try to see this statement as it will be seen by the committee. Is this a positive image? If so, what were the components that made it positive? If it was a negative image, what were the components that made it negative?

If you have had some research experience, this is the place to highlight those experiences. Don't just repeat what is in your resume. Spend time on the cover letter and statement of purpose. Make them shine and make them project you in a positive light as the very person they want to accept. This is where they can see your maturity and your skills with written English. This is also the information they need to try to fit or match your interests and the expertise of one or more faculty. If you've studied their catalogue (see **The interview** below) and know who the faculty are and what their interests are, you may be able to tailor your statement of purpose to fit well into the program of one or two faculty in whom you are particularly interested.

What are they looking for? More than likely, they are looking for maturity and a good match with their faculty interests.

Several final notes on your application: First, make absolutely certain that every application sent out is the very best that you can do. In your cover letter or statement of purpose, use a spell check, and if you are uncertain of your writing, have it edited by someone who is a practiced writer. It is advisable to send applications to a number of institutions. Make each application specific for the institution to which it is being sent.

Use the web; write for information; talk with your undergraduate faculty. In other words, do your homework for each institution! *Having done your homework, don't mess it up by using a generic application.* This is *very* important. Finally, do the follow-up necessary to make certain that all required pieces of your application have been received by the department to which you are applying.

The selection process.
You've sent in the best application possible. While you're waiting for a response, exactly what is happening? The department to which you have applied will have your application evaluated either

by an individual or a committee. In all probability, they will not read every piece of paper in your file. They will look at your GPA and GRE scores to establish that they are above the department minima. They will then read your cover letter and statement of purpose and from those documents; they will form an opinion of your writing ability and maturity. Next, they will read your letters of reference. If they know and respect one of your referees, that letter will be far more meaningful than if the letters are from three totally unknown people.

From these components, they will form an impression. Based on these impressions, all of the applications will be arranged into three stacks. In the first stack are the applications that are outstanding; in the third stack are the applications that will be rejected. In the second stack are those that will require more thought.

The students with outstanding applications constitute easy decisions. They will be interviewed and accepted and if at all possible, funding will be provided. The applications in the second stack will now be studied carefully to determine which if any of these will be considered for offers. The students with the better applications in this second stack will likely be interviewed and possibly accepted, but may not be funded their first year. The students with applications in the third stack also constitute easy decisions; they will receive polite rejection letters.

- What elements move an application from one stack to another?
- High grade point average.
- High Graduate Record Examination scores.
- Excellent letters of reference from people who are known to the department.

- Care in preparation.
- Maturity evident in the statement of purpose.
- A well-rounded background with thorough course work in the area of interest.
- A good match between your interests and the research programs in the department.
- Availability of funding.
- Demonstrated research performance in an internship.

In a very special set of circumstances, there is something more that you can do. If you particularly want acceptance by a specific department, and if one of the faculty who has agreed to write a letter on your behalf knows one or more faculty in that department, and if this faculty member is your enthusiastic supporter, he/she can call their contact in that department, tell them about you and alert them that your application is coming. This won't guarantee your acceptance but it will guarantee that your application will receive *very* careful attention.

The interview.
Most departments recognize that they will invest a tremendous amount of time, money and energy in graduate students, and that the quality of students graduating with advanced degrees from their department represents the department's future reputation. (For example, a science department may invest more than $100,000 in each Ph.D. student, so they are very careful with the admissions decisions!) For these reasons, they want to assess the students being accepted into their graduate program carefully and may well choose to interview the students prior to acceptance. It is particularly common for departments to interview applicants before offering funding.

In most cases, the student's travel and local expenses of the student being interviewed are covered by the department. Receiving an invitation for an interview means that you look good on paper. So, you have your foot in the door; to make certain that you present yourself well, you should do the following:

- **Do your homework.** Before the interview, read their catalog, use the web, and read any other materials you can obtain to get information about that department. Know who the members of the faculty are and what their fields of interest are.

- **Practice.** Get together with someone who has been through interviews in the academic world (faculty, graduate student, etc), and have them take you through a mock interview. Act as though they were interviewing you, and answer their questions as well as you can. If they ask you a question that stumps you, go off and think about it. The more thought you have given to your responses, the more polished your answers will be and the more mature you will appear during the interview.

Questions that might be asked of you during a mock interview are:

1. Would you tell me a bit about your background?
2. Why do you want to go to graduate school?
3. What research experiences have you had?
4. What career options are you considering following a graduate degree?
5. Why are you considering this institution for your graduate training?
6. What are your interests outside of the academic world?
7. What questions do you have for me?

Dress appropriately.
If any of the literature you have from that department includes photographs of graduate students, carefully note how they are dressed. If you dress slightly better than they are dressed, you will likely be appropriate. Don't under-dress. Remember, you want to project yourself as an academic. Probably the safest dress will be slacks or skirt at or below the knee, shirt, tie for men, casual or dress shoes (no sandals or sneakers), and coat or blazer. If you arrive at the department and discover that you are the only one dressed that well, you can easily dress-down by removing the tie and coat. (Think through ahead of time how you might dress-down.)

If you arrive in slacks and an open-necked shirt, and discover that all others are dressed in coat and tie, you do not have the option of dressing up. Some departments may expect suits for both men and women. When you are notified that the department would like to interview you, ask the department representative what the appropriate dress code is. **Don't** dress as if for a date. For both men and women, remember that this is an academic environment. You want to show off your intellectual capacity. Do not dress to show off your body. In this environment, you want to be judged based on what you know, not based on what you show. Don't wear much jewelry or use much makeup. Dress as an academic professional. You want the interviewers to see you as someone who will represent their department well. If this style of dress is not your typical attire, practice for several days with that particular outfit (particularly the shoes) before the interview. Maturity includes being comfortable with yourself, and that includes being comfortable with your clothing.

Maintain control.
You've heard of the good cop/bad cop routine. This is a routine in which one person takes a very hard and aggressive approach while

the second person takes a soft and calm approach. There is a similar interview technique. You may well find yourself at some time talking with someone who is extremely aggressive or quite negative. Be polite, listen carefully so that you can evaluate the situation before you respond, and consider the substance later, but **do not permit yourself to be "baited"** into excessively aggressive responses
Maintain control!
Stay positive!

Part of the interview process is designed to evaluate your maturity level. One of the characteristics of the mature person is knowledge of and confidence in self. Maintain a positive attitude, particularly if the conversation around you becomes negative. Don't permit yourself to become negative. Keep in mind that you are being interviewed, in part, to become a member of a small community. If you were already a member of that community, would you accept yourself based upon your performance in this interview?

Interview while being interviewed.
This is an excellent opportunity to inform yourself further about the environment in this department. Use it. Be inquisitive but **don't** be judgmental. Find out about the department and the people. Look at student offices, mail boxes, bulletin boards, etc. Is the environment active? Is the environment friendly? Talk informally with the graduate secretary about the program. This is the real repository of information. He/she typically knows a great deal about the program, and knows where to go to ask for information. Don't draw conclusions yet, but gather as much information as possible.

Be very reluctant to drink.
If you are invited out and are offered an alcoholic drink, the safest course of action is to politely decline the drink. If you normally

drink alcoholic beverages, and if everyone else is drinking, accept *one* and "nurse it" for the evening. The classic place to lose the interview is after having too much to drink. Don't kid yourself. We are **all** affected by alcohol. You will **not** perform as well if you drink. The only question is how much is too much for you in this particular situation? If you are out with a group of graduate students and all are drinking, you will be in a difficult situation. As you are making your decision, keep in mind that this is still part of the interview. If you decline to drink, it may be viewed that you won't fit in. On the other hand, if your performance is negatively impacted by alcohol, it may be viewed that your intellect is below that of the other students. Our recommendation: if you feel that you must drink, do so in very careful and deliberate moderation.

Follow-up after the interview:
Once you're back home, within several days, send a short letter to the chairperson or the admissions committee director thanking the department for the opportunity to visit and indicating your continued interest in graduate opportunities in the department. You've learned a lot about that department and you may have learned about a particular research program into which you think you would fit. Indicate your interest in this program in your letter. Also, following the interview, make some notes on the positives and negatives and make your own assessment of whether or not this department is the best place for you to pursue a graduate degree.

Always be aware that you may be "on interview":
One of the authors (KLP) several years ago received a phone call from an individual who indicated that she was conducting a "survey" for her company at the request of organization "X." She indicated that she would like to pose questions designed to obtain the author's opinions concerning the operation of organization "X." She proceeded to ask a long series of questions concerning

this particular organization. Interestingly, the author had recently informally let this organization know of his interest in working with that group. Thus, this "survey" was not a survey. Rather, it was an interview thinly disguised as a survey.

The authors have also experienced finishing an interview with a particular institution, and then, on the journey home, being engaged in a seemingly innocent conversation with an individual who eventually turns out to be an official of the institution. These two stories underscore the possibility that you may not know that you are on interview. Many of the interviews of life are not formal. They may take place during a survey; they may take place at a party. Be safe! <u>Always</u> behave as though you are on interview.

Sample cover letters:
As you read these sample letters, imagine that **you** are on the admissions committee, and consider the impression that the letter makes on you as an admissions committee member.

Cover letter 1:

Dr. J. Brown
Chair, Department of Biology
Somewhere University
Centerville, Mid-America

Dear Dr. Brown:

      I am enclosing my application for graduate school in the Department of Biology.

Sincerely,
Hopeful Candidate

Authors' analysis: This letter fulfills the formal need for a cover letter while otherwise adding absolutely nothing of value to your file. It is a waste of paper.

Cover letter 2:

Dr. J. Brown
Chair, Department of Biology,
Somewhere University
Centerville, Mid-America

Dear Dr. Brown:

I am interested in and wish to be considered as a candidate for a PhD program in the Department of Biology.

I have been deeply interested in the study of biology since I was a small child, and that interest has been sharpened by my experiences as an undergraduate at Podunck College. In particular, I worked as a volunteer intern in the laboratory of Dr. Mary House during my junior year. As I learned the techniques used in Dr. House's laboratory, I was allowed to conduct my own experiments on the purification of radish hexokinase under the direction of Dr. Jim Jones, a post-doctoral research associate for Dr. House. This research provided me with the opportunity to learn that I truly love laboratory research, and that I wish ultimately to direct myself toward a research career.

In my weekly discussions with Dr. House, she has encouraged me to consider pursuing a PhD in your Department of Biology. Based on the papers I have read from several of your faculty, my interests at present are focused on the research programs of Drs. Allan, Beet, and Handsuch, although I may find that my interests will broaden as I learn more about the research programs in the Department.

My application for admission into the PhD program is enclosed, and Drs. House, Tweety, and Banks have been asked to send you letters on my behalf.

Thank you very much for your consideration.

Sincerely,
Hopeful Candidate

Authors' analysis: This letter tells a great deal about the candidate, and, by demonstrating the candidate's evident maturity, considerable raises the probability that the entire file will be carefully read by the Chair and by the admissions committee.

Sample statements of purpose:

As you read these sample statements, imagine that **you** are on the admissions committee, and consider the impression that the statement makes on you as an admissions committee member.

Statement of Purpose 1:

I am 22 years old. I have 2 older brothers and 2 yunger sisters. My father is a computer analyst. my mother is a libarian. I have always liked being around plants and animals. My grades in science have been good so I might as well be a scientist. I am active in my church, and my sorority. I was a finalist for Homecoming Queen. I was runner up, and was in the Court. I am active at the gym, and have a brown belt in karate. I like TV and movies. I am attractive and have a good personality. I think that a graduate degree will prepare me for a better life. I think that yours is a good University and was impressed by its Basketball Team and "Final Four" appearance. I would like for my next degree to be from a Championship University like yours.

Authors' analysis: This statement of purpose is a very loud advertisement of immaturity. The sentences are short and choppy; there are several misspellings, the grammar is poor, and there is much information that is simply not relevant. It is unlikely that the file of this student will receive further attention.

Statement of Purpose 2:

I have always excelled in school and everything else that I have tried. I found the sciences to be extraordinarily interesting and made excellent marks in all of my science classes. I performed well in inorganic and organic chemistry, physics and biology. I built my own computer and have proficiency in most of the common software programs. I am also a member of the band, playing drums, and am in the musical choral at my school. I thought I might want to live in Europe so joined the French Club and German Club. In my spare time, I am a stamp collector.

In considering my career options late in my senior year, I considered those areas in which I was very good, and those areas where jobs might be plentiful. Based on these considerations, I think that I might be willing to consider a graduate degree in science such as molecular biology, biochemistry, pharmacology, veterinary medicine or even human medicine. Since your institution is famous in these areas, I thought I would consider getting a doctorate degree there.

I will appreciate hearing from you as soon as possible regarding which programs I have been accepted and funded by. Send me information on these programs, and I will than be able to decide which program to pursue.

Authors' analysis: The impression given by the applicant writing this statement is one of arrogance. This person is not interested in being either guided or taught. He/she is solely interested in being famous. It would be a rare department that would accept such an applicant.

Statement of Purpose 3:

Since I was a small boy, I have been interested in the sciences, and particularly in biology. My father is a veterinarian as is my older sister, so my early interest in biology was primarily focused on animals. This interest was demonstrated by science fair participation and membership in 4H as a teenager. Through these activities, I developed a love for the outdoors, and spend much of my recreational time camping and hiking in various ecological habitats.

Knowing that a career in biology would require a college degree and possibly a graduate degree, I have taken a variety of courses in the sciences. Last spring, at the end of my sophomore year in college, I took a course in wetland ecology from Dr. B. Mused and was fascinated to learn of the many complexities of plants and plant interactions. At that point, I decided that I wanted to direct my career toward plant biology.

I also have been quite interested by the area of molecular genetics. In a seminar course, I discovered that many of the exciting innovations in molecular genetics are actually being developed in plant molecular biology. I have read a number of papers written in this area by the faculty at your university, and based on these and your course offerings, wish to pursue a PhD degree in Plant Breeding and Genetics in your department. I am particularly interested in working in a research area in which I can explore moving genes from one plant to another with the goal of increasing plant productivity.

Following completion of my graduate studies, I would like to work in some environment, whether University, Government or Industry, in which I can direct my skills as a plant molecular biologist to feeding our world's growing population. I see myself directing and conducting research, but also see myself actively involved in training young plant molecular biologists.

I appreciate your consideration of my application and look forward to hearing from the Program in Plant Breeding and Genetics.

Authors' analysis: This is a well-balanced statement. It demonstrates thought and is well-written. It is highly likely that the applicant will be seriously considered for acceptance.

Statement of Purpose 4:

As a junior in the Eisenhower Magnet High School, I was accepted into a summer program for gifted and talented students at the College here in Podunck. I proposed an exciting project to my mentor on a mathematical model for determining enzymatic activity of proteins. In spite of my confidence that this project would result in a Westinghouse Talent Search Scholarship, my mentor directed my entire summer toward the isolation and purification of a single enzyme, which for purely technical reasons was not successful. In spite of this, I obtained a partial scholarship at Podunck, and am completing my B.S. in biochemistry.

I have read many of the papers of Dr. H. Nu, Professor in Biochemistry, and wish to work with Professor Nu. Given his work and reputation on protein structure, I am confident that I can

24

now develop the mathematical model for determining enzyme activity using the data on enzyme activity available in the Rutgers University Data Base known at PDB. I feel totally confident that my work will lead to a Nobel Prize for me and Professor Nu.

After completion of my degree, I think that an endowed chair in biochemistry will permit me direct my efforts in research, further refining and extending this model.

This application should be forwarded to Professor Nu so that I can begin and thus complete my work as quickly as possible.

Authors' analysis: Similar to statement 2 above, this statement comes across as being from a very self-centered and arrogant person. The student is not interested in being educated or mentored. He/she is solely interested in a place where he/she can become famous. It would be a rare department that would accept such an applicant.

Caution:
Never under any circumstances should your cover letter and statement of purpose not be your own work. It may be tempting to have someone else write these for you. **Don't do it!** It will be evident on interview that these are not your own work, and no Department will accept a student who uses as their own someone else's work.

*F*unding sources

You've just completed or are close to completing your undergraduate degree, and if you're like most students, you have supported the expenses of your undergraduate education by working during the summers, working part time at school, being subsidized by parents, and by "student loans." If you have been very fortunate, you have also received financial assistance in the form of a scholarship from your institutions. By putting all of these together, you've been able to meet your institutional expenses, have a roof over your head and food on your table, and have some social life. You are probably not anxious to continue to eke out a living like this, and you may be receiving some very subtle pressure from parents to find a job. Thus, the financial component exerts considerable pressure on your decision of whether or not you should go to graduate school for an advanced degree.

You need to be aware that funding may be available for over half of the students enrolled in graduate school. At the Ph.D. level, usually more than 80-90% of the students have some form of support. For Master's students it may be less. These numbers depend on the field of study. With this funding, you will likely be expected to work, but that work typically will be in your professional area, and not flipping burgers in a fast food restaurant. You will not be wealthy, but you should be able to direct your attention to your studies, and not spend all of your time fighting off the wolves at the door, or begging from your patient parents. Three general sources of funding are available. You should carefully investigate the availability of all three.

Fellowships:
Your chosen institution will usually have some funds available for the partial support of graduate students in the form of fellowships. Fellowships typically carry no duties or obligations, but frequently specify a minimum performance (typically, a minimum GPA) level. This minimum performance level should be no real problem for a student with enough drive to be in graduate school. For information on fellowships, you should inquire at the graduate school or at the department to which you are applying.
Funding is frequently available to members of many specific groups. For example you may find funding available if you are the daughter of the member of a particular sorority. You may find funding if you are from a farming family in the southeastern part of a particular state. Funding may be available if you are the third oldest son from a father who is a retired plumber. At times these groups appear quite irrational, but these funding sources should definitely be explored.

One funding source available to members of specific groups is quite rational. In most institutions of higher learning in the United States, it is openly acknowledged, at least by the administration, that the quality of education experienced by all students is higher if the institution is culturally diverse. Exposure to cultural diversity challenges the student's intellectual growth and better prepares the student for the workforce in a global and culturally diverse community. For this reason, many institutions offer fellowships to students who represent populations that have been historically under-represented from the higher education process such as African Americans, Latino Americans, Native Americans, women or students with disabilities. If you represent a historically under-represented group, be certain that you inquire about such fellowships.

Note that the availability of such funding does **not** guarantee your admission to the institution. You are accepted based on ability, not based on your membership in a historically under-represented population. However, once admitted for graduate study, explore the availability of such funding, knowing that this will assist you toward your graduate degree, and that your presence on that campus will increase its diversity and thus improve the quality of education for all.

A number of States have made fellowships based on race or ethnicity illegal. Many institutions in such States still have such fellowships when they are funded by gifts to the institution, and the gift specified such a basis on race or ethnicity. Many of these institutions also offer fellowships based on the unique background that an individual from an under-represented population may bring to the institution. For example, individuals from under-represented populations may be the first in their family to pursue a graduate degree, or be from a migrant farm worker family. Consider carefully what you bring to the institution that may not otherwise be represented without including race or ethnicity.

Teaching assistantships:
As a candidate for an advanced degree, you will probably be required to teach or assist with the teaching of at least one undergraduate course, and funds may be available to support this service to the department. This experience will provide an excellent opportunity for you to learn *how to teach*. If you want ultimately to teach at any level, the need to learn how to teach is crucial, and should be evident. The ability to teach is not conferred with a Ph.D., rather, it is learned. Keep in mind that the ability to teach is useful far beyond K-20 education. Most professional opportunities have some component of teaching whether it be the training of one or of many individuals.

The teaching assistantship will typically require that you provide a teaching service to the department of about 12-20 hours *per* week. This may include your time before the class, office hours, and preparation time. In return for this service to the department, you will receive support which typically may include payment for at least some of the courses you take that term, and a stipend. The amount of the stipend is typically set by the department or university and cannot be negotiated. Note that the stipend is subject to federal and state taxes.

Ask whether or not a tuition waiver for courses and/or fees and student health insurance are included as part of the support. The stipend is usually sufficient to support housing, food, clothing and *some* travel. In other words, the stipend will support a modest lifestyle. You aren't likely to save much money, but you aren't likely to need an outside supplement either.

The advantages of a teaching assistantship are that it supports teaching that you may be required to do anyway, and that you are being paid for work in your chosen profession. The disadvantage is that the assistantship takes time which must be spent in addition to that required for your own courses and that required for your research. To find out about the availability of teaching assistantships, let the department know that you need funding for your graduate studies and that you wish to be considered for a teaching assistantship.

Research assistantship:
You will be expected to submit a thesis or dissertation for your advanced degree. This describes your own research. If you elect to work with a research advisor who is funded for his/her research program from an outside agency such as the federal government or a private foundation, that advisor may well have funding to support you to work on your research project within his/her research program.

Such a research assistantship is typically equivalent to the amount of money you could expect from a teaching assistantship, and will frequently include some support for the courses you take that term. Ask whether or not a tuition waiver/fees and student health insurance are included as part of the support. Again, you won't be wealthy, but you won't starve either.

The advantages of a research assistantship are that it supports the research that you are required to do for your thesis or dissertation, and that you are being paid for work in your chosen profession. The disadvantage is that the assistantship may constrain your research project. That is, your research project *must* fit into the research program of your research advisor. Under most circumstances, this will be of no consequence. In the rare case, when your research takes you into a new direction, this option may not be funded under the constraints of the funded research program. Notice that this describes the importance of a good match between your interests and the research programs of the faculty.

Under some circumstances, you may be offered a research assistantship for work in a funded research program unrelated to your own research project. In this case, you are being paid for your research efforts, and you then must accomplish your own research in addition to the research for which you are funded. To find out about the availability of research assistantships, let the department know that you need funding for your graduate studies and that you wish to be considered for a research assistantship.

Obtain your own funding:
Literally thousands of programs are available in this country supporting graduate education. Go to your library and explore on line, use the databases, and find out more about such programs. Choose those for which you seem qualified and apply. If you can obtain your own funding, it will tremendously increase your attractiveness to any department to which you may be applying. Number one, this indicates that you have taken the initiative on your own (viewed as one component of maturity) to obtain funding. Number two, this indicates that an outside group has found you to be *worthy* of funding, Number three, because you have outside funding, you will not compete for the limited departmental funds.

Federal loans:
If you are a U.S. citizen or permanent resident, you may apply for loans, just as you may have as an undergraduate. Many graduate students supplement their fellowship or assistantship with a loan. The Office of Financial Aid at your institution can advise you on

this process and most have a website devoted to this source of funds.

In some institutions, the majority of master's students and a substantial fraction of PhD students use loans in addition to the other funding sources from their department or institution.

In summary, it is likely that you can find financial support for your graduate studies. This support may be in the form of a fellowship, but is more likely to be in the form of a teaching assistantship or research assistantship.

Explore **all** of the possibilities!

IV

*O*verview of Your
Next Several Years

So you're considering embarking on a journey of at least several years duration in graduate school. A number of mile markers will be passed during this journey. Ahead of you, this can look quite formidable. However, by looking at this path, you will see that the hurdles are spaced out over time, and this makes the journey considerably easier. What will the path look like? Although we can't say with certainty, we can come up with a generalized map. Two such maps will be presented in this section. Because the master's program and Ph.D. program may be rather different, they will be covered separately, and note will be made of several connectors between the two programs. In addition, there are at least two different varieties of master's programs, the course work master's program and the research master's program. These will be covered separately.

Coursework master's program:

This is frequently thought of as the "coursework" master's program, and typically consists of the next logical set of courses in a particular field beyond the bachelor's level. In some professional fields, these courses may be required to maintain licenses or to prepare for certain specific careers. Examples can be found in business administration, criminal justice, education, labor and industrial relations, allied health areas including nursing, and social work. Typically such a program will consist of a series of courses taken in a specified order over one to two years. There may be little flexibility for the student to design his/her own specific program.

The coursework master's program differs from the research master's program in that the courses represent the vast majority of work required for the program and the rigor in that program. In additional, the student is typically not supported financially through the coursework master's program. In contrast, in the research master's program, the research required for the thesis represents the major amount of work and rigor in the program.

While there may be research involved in the coursework master's program, that research is often contained within the component courses. Thus, research papers may be required, but a research thesis is not required. In part because there is less emphasis on research, there may also be less individual contact with faculty, so less opportunity to learn professional skills from a formal mentor. In a few cases, the coursework master's degree is awarded as a

36

terminal degree to the student who has been unable to successfully complete the program for a research master's degree or a Ph.D. degree.

Research master's program:
The beginning of your research master's program will be spent almost entirely on course work. It is important that you choose a research advisor no later than the beginning of your second term, and an advisory committee as soon as possible thereafter. Once your advisor and committee have been selected, your research and course requirements can be established. Because this should happen as quickly as possible, the selection of advisor and committee must not be delayed. It is likely that the course work will take two years, and that the research component will be added at least by your second term. For a master's degree, the research thesis is typically regarded as an introduction to research; and in the sciences and engineering, some or much of the project design may be done by your advisor. The results of your research may be expected to constitute the manuscript for approximately one publication in a research journal.

In addition to course work and research, you may be required to teach a single course to fulfill one of your degree requirements, and you may be required to pass a final or qualifying examination (see section **XV**), which would be administered probably at the end of the program. The length of time for a master's degree is variable but is typically one to three years beyond a bachelor's degree. Toward the end of your research master's program, you will spend up to two months writing your thesis (see section **XVI)** which, following editing, will be approved by your advisor. Following defense of your thesis (see section **XVI**), your advisory committee will decide on a "pass," "additional work is necessary," or "no pass." If the decision is "pass," the committee will typically also choose to suggest that you pursue a Ph.D., or that you stop with the master's degree.

In many departments, there are several points at which a person can move from a research master's program into a Ph.D. program. The first of these is upon completion of the qualifying exam, if used by the department. A second point may come toward the end of the second year, when the successful student may be encouraged to bypass the master's degree, continue research and pursue a Ph.D. degree.

The advantage of a research master's program is the relatively short period of time required, and low number of requirements. The disadvantage, if you will eventually pursue a Ph.D., is that the combination of a research master's degree and Ph.D. typically takes longer than the Ph.D. alone. In addition, following the research master's degree, the student may need to go back through the application process to be accepted into a Ph.D. program. On the other hand, many people regard a research master's degree as good preparation for a Ph.D. program, particularly for the student who is a "late bloomer." Both of the authors were considered "late bloomers," and completed master's degrees before pursuing the Ph.D.

Ph.D. program:
Receipt of a Ph.D. is a statement from the institution that you are a skilled practitioner of research in your discipline. This is a research degree. However, having said that, it is rare that a Ph.D. program consists only of research. At the beginning of your first year, most of your time will be spent on course work. During this time, especially in the biological or biomedical sciences, you may also do "rotations" with various potential advisors (see section **VI**), or begin your research efforts under your chosen advisor. In any case, most of your early effort will be directed toward your course

work. You will choose your research advisor or be chosen by a research advisor, and work toward the choice of your advisory committee by the end of your first year. As with the research master's program, it is important that you choose a research advisor and advisory committee as quickly as possible, because these choices must precede the setting of your course requirements. Note that you may end up choosing a research advisor after already enrolling and possibly completing some of your course work. Typically, for this reason, it is recommended that the course work your first term consist of "core" courses that you would need to take regardless of which research advisor you select.

Your course work will likely be completed within two or slightly more years. When you have completed most of your course work, you will schedule, study for, and complete your comprehensive examination (see section **XV**). Following successful completion of your comprehensive examination, you will spend most of your time on your research. Your research project will usually begin largely as a study directed by your advisor (so similar to a "master's" research program), but by the end of your Ph.D., your research should be almost entirely independent and "in consultation with" your advisor. The results of your research may be expected to constitute a book or several manuscripts for journal papers. You should *seriously* consider attending and giving presentations at professional meetings also. These meetings are the arenas for discussions by academics. You need to become active in the coliseum (arena) of your profession.

In addition to course work and research, you may be required to teach in several courses to fulfill one of your degree requirements, and you may be required to pass a qualifying examination (see section **XIV**), which would be administered probably at the end of your first year. In addition, the comprehensive exam (or "comps") is (are) an integral part of most Ph.D. programs. This (these) is (are) completed at the end of coursework and may also include a dissertation research proposal that you defend. The Ph.D. may take you from three to ten years to complete, depending upon your discipline although the average is from three to six years. You, your research advisor, and advisory committee will establish goals for your research early in your program.

As you approach completion of those goals, you will be encouraged by your advisor and committee to begin the writing of your dissertation. This will usually take two to four months (see section **XVI)**. Following approval of the dissertation by your advisor, the dissertation will be submitted to your committee. Following defense of your dissertation which often has a formal, open seminar requirement (see section **XVI**), your advisory committee will decide for a "pass," "additional work is necessary," or "no pass." It is hoped that your preparation will be sufficient that a "no pass" will not be considered. However, if your performance is judged to be inadequate on your comprehensive examination, or possibly on your defense, some institutions may encourage that you leave the graduate program with a master's degree.

The length of time for a PhD is variable, but is seldom less than three years or more than 10 years beyond a bachelor's degree. The shorter times are more typical in the natural and physical sciences; the longer times are more typical in the arts and letters, social sciences and education. At the end of the Ph.D., you are awarded a degree, which is the highest accolade of success in the academic world. Perhaps more than any other hurdle, this degree signifies that you are one of the relatively few people trained in research and capable of independent pursuit of knowledge and its dissemination.

U

An Explicit Statement of the Implicit Rules for Success in the Academic Community

In every community, whether that community is a religious community, business community, high school community, academic community or other, there are unwritten rules that govern the behavior of the members of that community. For example in a particular church, there may be an unwritten rule that men should wear a coat and tie in the church service and shake hands upon meeting another man. These rules may be so deeply ingrained that obedience of the rules is simply assumed to constitute appropriate behavior, and that the presence of the rule, itself, is not noticed by the community member.

If one were to ask members of that community about unwritten rules, most would respond that there are no rules. However, adherence to these rules easily distinguishes the community member (insider) from the visitor (outsider). Frequently, the community member does not see non-adherence to these rules as non-adherence to a rule but rather as *truly* inappropriate behavior. Thus the outsider may be viewed as a person who is not simply an outsider but as beneath consideration for membership in the community. Thus, it can easily be seen that knowledge of the unwritten rules can be extremely important.

There are three unwritten rules for inclusion in most components of the academic community. As in other communities, most members of the academic community would claim that such rules do not exist, or would suggest that the sole criterion for inclusion is the individual's intelligence. However, non-adherence to these rules will typically result not only in being seen as an outsider to the academic community, but in being viewed as inappropriate for inclusion because of *lacking intelligence*. This can be tragic because the rule is little, if at all, related to intelligence.

Based on the experiences of the authors, the three major unwritten rules for inclusion in the academic community are: *promptness, display of a work ethic*, and *professional behavior*. Having said that, take a moment to think back to your application. One of the major factors in your application and in the interview process was your maturity. Well, maturity continues to be important, and it plays out in your responses to the three rules.

Be prompt:
In most sectors of the academic community in the United States, time is viewed as an extremely important commodity, and is not to be wasted. The wasting of another person's time by arriving late for a meeting or appointment has a very low tolerance level. Nine o'clock am means nine o'clock am, not ten minutes after nine. If you are late, apologize. Don't pretend that you were on time. To demonstrate a lack of respect for another person's time is frequently interpreted as lacking respect for their work, and that is assumed to happen only if one does not have the intellect to understand that work. Thus, if you are consistently late, you will be viewed as not caring, and in the academic community, ***this will likely be equated with lack of mental prowess.***

Note that promptness includes the prompt or early application for admission into the graduate program. Some departments will automatically reject any late application.

Display a work ethic:
Membership in the academic community is limited regardless of rank (professor, research associate, or graduate student). Funding is also limited. Most people in the community are there because the process of acquiring knowledge excites them. You will be expected to share this excitement. If you are lazy, you will be viewed as lacking commitment or not caring, and as above, this is equated with lack of mental prowess. This does not mean that you cannot have a life outside of academia. It does mean that you cannot be a clock-watcher, and that you ***enthusiastically*** embrace additional responsibilities. (Note the emphasis on enthusiasm.) Two additional characteristics go into your work ethic: resilience and tenacity. Can you in fact alter your path when it is required? Can you accept constructive criticism without being devastated? Are you a self-starter? Do you cling to the task even when it becomes very difficult or even routine?

Be a professional:
The typical full-time undergraduate student spends most of his/her time in his/her dormitory room or apartment. From there, the student goes off to class, or the library, etc, and after completing that particular mission, returns to his/her room. After classes are over for the term, or during spring break, the student typically leaves campus to go to their parents' home or to take a holiday/vacation. The full-time graduate student is <u>expected</u> to display a very different work pattern. If the graduate student has a desk in his/her academic department or even in the space of their research advisor, they will be expected to use this as an "office".

On a typical day, the student will leave his/her room or apartment early in the morning for their "office," and from there go to class, the library, etc, and then back to his/her "office." They will study there and in general put in a full workday at their "office." If you cannot obtain "office" space in your department, try to find its equivalent in the library (a study Carrel), or establish a rather formal "office" at home. Having an office helps one maintain a professional schedule. At the end of the term or over spring break, the student will use most of the time on his/her research, trying to accomplish those tasks for which there was inadequate time during the term.

This does not mean that the graduate student cannot take off for holiday/vacation time, but the amount of such time is rarely as much as 3-4 weeks *per* year. (Typically, the amount of time for vacation for a graduate student will be about 2 weeks *per* year.) Notice that the *behavior pattern of the full-time graduate student is centered on his/her work place*, while that of the full-time undergraduate student is centered on their living or vacationing place. If the graduate student does not display this graduate student behavior, frequently even if the student's work is being

44

accomplished, the student will be viewed as *lacking commitment to their profession* and a lack of commitment to the profession is unprofessional.

Are there any other rules? Yes, there probably are other unwritten rules that are specific to your own institution or department. For example, there may be an unwritten dress code. How do you find out about these rules? In large part, you will find out by carefully observing others in your community. If you are fortunate enough to have a mentor who studies his/her own culture, they may volunteer to become an "informed insider," making such implicit rules explicit.

Does this mean that you must change who you are? Only you can answer that question. You likely already have multiple behaviors that you use in different places. For example, you likely behave differently in your faith community, on the sports field, or out with your boy friend/girl friend. Yet all of these behaviors are you. Each additional behavior is an additional tool in your behavioral toolbox as you move across cultural boundaries. If you wish to be included in your academic community, and thereby maximize the probabilities of your academic success, you will carefully consider the unwritten rules of the academic community.

For a delightfully creative alternative to working completely submerged in any institutional environment, see:
MacKenzie, G. 1998. *Orbiting the giant hairball. A corporate fool's guide to surviving with grace.* Penguin Books. N.Y., N. Y.

VI

*C*hoosing a Research Advisor

Parable of the rabbit and her dissertation. *Once upon a time in a time close to now and in a land not too far away, a small rabbit sat outside her burrow, deeply engrossed in writing on her laptop computer. A fox spotted the rabbit and interpreting this as an easy meal, sauntered up to the rabbit, asking what she was doing. Upon being told that* *she was writing her dissertation about how rabbits eat foxes, the fox indicated that this was ridiculous. The rabbit offered to prove it and invited the fox into her burrow. Shortly, the rabbit reappeared and went back to work. A bit later this same scene was repeated as a wolf saw the rabbit. Much the same conversation transpired, and soon, the rabbit and wolf disappeared into her burrow with the wolf licking his lips. As before, only the rabbit reappeared.*

Inside of the burrow, unknown to the outside world, there was a large pile of fox and wolf bones, but in addition, half of the burrow was occupied by the rabbit's "research advisor," a large lion with a full stomach.

The moral of this story is that it really doesn't matter what you choose for a thesis topic, or what your thesis purports to show. It is enormously important to carefully choose your research advisor.

(ADAPTED FROM:"A RABBIT'S THESIS" http://www.patsjokes.com/education/rabbit_thesis. html)

The single most important part of this story is its moral. The choice of your research mentor is one of the central choices you have to make - more important by far than the choice of institution or department. This is especially true for research master's and Ph.D. students! This is the single person who will guide you on a substantial portion of your intellectual journey in graduate school, who will then open doors for you professionally, and whose reputation will be enhanced because you chose to have your research work directed by them. The importance of your research mentor will continue long after your graduation as you request letters of reference for positions. How can one go about making a decision this important? What should the student look for?

Research topic:
This may be just exactly the research topic that excites you. You simply can't imagine working on anything other than this particular topic. If so, you should very seriously consider working with this person. However, keep in mind all that you have heard about the high probability that a person will change careers multiple times in their lifetime. The same is true for one's research area. It is relatively rare for a person to continue working throughout their professional career on the same research topic. So, it really is not all that important to decide now what **topic** you want to work on for the rest of your career. More importantly, is this research topic one about which you are sufficiently excited to work on for possibly as much as the next five years. The research topic is important but not as the *only* basis for a decision. Read on!

Track record:
You would like to know how many students have been successfully guided by this person in the past. It is perfectly appropriate to ask the person for a list of past and present students and to directly contact these past and present students asking for their assessment of the interaction they had with the person. If possible, do this by phone or in person, and not by mail or e-mail. In person or by phone, you have the opportunity to assess the value of the information by watching the non-verbal (body) language or listening to subtle voice tones. These may guide your interaction and questions. Don't try to put the person on the spot, but listen "between-the-lines" for feelings. One question that should always be asked is: "If you had this to do over, would you

make the same decision?" Other questions might be: "What percent of students who started with this mentor actually complete his/her program?" "What was the time-to-degree?" "What were the person's strengths as an advisor/mentor? What were the person's weaknesses as an advisor/mentor?" "Were you encouraged to make presentations at professional meetings and to submit manuscripts to journals?" Seldom is there anyone so weak that they have no strengths, but seldom also is there anyone so strong that they have no weaknesses. If you're told only of strengths or only of weaknesses, you may want to seriously question that person's assessment. Conscientiously hold all information received in complete confidence. Try to determine the person's management and communication style (see below) from past students also.

Professional stature:
What is the professional stature of the research advisor you are considering? How does one assess this? First, talk with faculty in your present institution and get their assessment about the professional stature of the person. Second, go to the Peterson's Guide (begin your search of Peterson's Guides by going to www.petersons.com) to determine who is in the department and to get some feeling for the ranking of that department. Go to the literature in your field and check under that person's name to determine their publication record. Look in other papers or books on similar topics to determine whether or not that person's papers or books are being cited by other researchers in the field. What awards do they have? (e.g., are they a member of the National Academy of Sciences or another similar organization?)

Avoid the temptation to evaluate the person beyond your data set. You are assessing professional stature only. This is not the only characteristic to be assessed. For example, a young faculty member may simply be too new in the profession to have achieved a major stature. This does not mean that this person would be a poor research advisor. It may mean that this person will have less clout when it comes to pushing you for a position, etc. On the other hand, the person with great professional stature may be a poor mentor simply because of being too busy with professional commitments to devote time to you.

Management and communication style:
Each of us has a management and communication style with which we prefer to work. Think about your past interactions with teachers, mentors, supervisors, etc. What were their styles of management and communication? With which of these did you feel most comfortable? Were there any styles with which you simply could not work? Now, seek to assess the management and communication style of the person with whom you are considering working. It is appropriate to ask them this question, but most faculty members likely won't know how to answer the question. It is appropriate and far more informative to ask others who know them, including their past and present students. Are your preferred style and their preferred styles in conflict? For example, if you have a need for face-to-face meetings, then you might be quite uncomfortable with a research advisor who prefers to communicate with you via e-mail memos even though you occupy the same office or laboratory space. On the other hand, if you prefer communication through memos or email, you might be uncomfortable with a research advisor who prefers daily face-to-face communication.

Funding:
(See III above.) In many areas of academia, support for the Ph.D. graduate student is derived primarily from the student's work on a research project for which the research advisor has funding. Such funding would not only cover the supplies and travel required for the research but would also fund the support stipend for the

student. It should then be evident that electing to work for an advisor who lacks funding might seriously hinder the progress of the student's research. How do you find out about funding? Ask the potential research advisor.

When is the decision on research advisor made? The answer largely depends on the department. In some cases, the student may be accepted by the department, begin their studies and during their first term have the opportunity to make this decision. In other departments, the research advisor may need to be chosen before the student begins their study. In the best of all cases, a department will accept and fund the student, and permit them several "rotations" during their first term or two, but this is largely an option only in the biological or biomedical sciences.

The rotation is a short work experience with a potential research advisor. It permits a mutual evaluation by the faculty member and student, and it permits the student to briefly explore an area of research that they might otherwise not experience. (Note that the rotation is typically not intended to produce a publication.) In other cases, following acceptance of a student by a department, the student may be approached by a faculty member who has funding and asked if they would like to consider working in the faculty member's particular (funded) research program. Whatever the path, the student should obtain as much information as possible about the potential advisor before making a decision.

In summary, a number of factors should be considered in making the decision to work with a particular person as research advisor. Use **all** of these factors. **No single factor should automatically be assumed to be paramount.**

VII

Course Work

As indicated above, one of the three important components of your application for graduate school is your transcript with record of courses taken and performance in those courses. You will need to take additional course work for an advanced degree under any but the most exceptional circumstances. Your course workload will generally be much less than that you became accustomed to as an undergraduate student. However, you will probably find the courses individually to be much more demanding and the amount of required reading to be much, much greater. Ironically, while your performance in the required course work must meet a minimum standard, your grades in course work will generally not be the major criterion of your success or failure in graduate school unless you are in a course work master's program.

Deciding on courses:
Soon after you begin graduate school, you will meet with your academic advisor to set up a plan of study for your first term. If you already have a research advisor, this person will typically also be your academic advisor. If you do not yet have a research advisor, another person will typically be appointed by the department as your interim academic advisor. In many cases, this person will be the departmental graduate advisor. Several factors will determine which courses you take.

- Your academic background. Have you completed all of the courses typically required for full admission into this department? If not, you may now have to take these additional courses.
- Department requirements. Many departments require completion of certain "core" courses by all of their graduate students.
- Your professional career goals. What degree are you working toward? What is your career objective? Ideally, you wish to position yourself such that you are on the "cutting edge" not just at the time of your degree, but also throughout your career. Give yourself the preparation that will permit this.
- Course availability. Not all courses are offered every term or even every year.

Course load:

A typical undergraduate course load may be 13-18 semester credits. In graduate school, a typical course load may be 6-9 semester credits. Hang on! Don't cheer yet! Remember that in addition to your course work, you may also be a teaching assistant for 20 hours per week, and be expected to be working on your research for an additional 20 hours per week. Using the old "rule of thumb" that one should study two hours outside of class for every hour in class, a six-credit load translates into a minimum of 18 hours of work per week (six hours in class and 12 hours outside of class). This adds up to a minimum weekly workload of 58 hours for a six-credit load, teaching duties and research duties.

In most universities, there are two levels of courses, undergraduate courses and graduate courses. You may need to take one or more undergraduate courses to fill in your background. These courses will be quite similar to those you have already experienced. However, much of your course work will be graduate courses. In such courses, the subject area is typically more focused, the class size may be smaller, and the expectation exists that you will learn a significant portion of the original literature in that area. Thus, you may use original papers rather than textbooks in many graduate courses. Assessment of your performance may be far more inventive than in an undergraduate course. Frequently, assessment includes activities normally expected of the successful professional in that area. For example, you may find that your grade depends heavily on written papers or research projects, oral presentations of your research on an assigned topic, written research proposals, or even oral examinations.

Grades:

Every graduate school has a set of minimum performance standards to remain in graduate school. Find out specifically what your graduate school standards are. In general, the student is warned and placed on probation following any final course grade below a 3.0 on a 0.0-4.0 scale, or if the grade point average falls below a 3.0. Several final course grades below 3.0 may result in **automatic** dismissal from the graduate school. Now, having said this, for the vast majority of graduate students, these minimum standards present no problem. But, a warning is appropriate. This is a new paradigm! As an undergraduate, you concentrated in large part on grades. Good grades were a significant part of your ticket into graduate school. Good grades are often *not* the most important ticket into your profession.

Following your graduate degree, your research, teaching skills, recommendations from mentors, *etc.* are the major tickets into your profession. So, maintain a balance. You have a number of areas in which you must perform in graduate school. One is course work. Are grades important? Yes! The student with the higher GPA may be offered the teaching assistantship. With all other thing equal, the student with the higher GPA may be preferentially accepted into a Ph.D. program. Maintain your performance safely above the minimum standards. Perform as well as you can in your course work. But *do not neglect your other duties*.

VIII

Choosing and Using an Advisory Committee

Following the choice of a research advisor, one of your most important decisions will be the people who will be on your advisory committee. Why is this group so important? These are the people whose signatures will show that your submitted thesis or dissertation meets the requirements for the Master's or Ph.D. degree. Now, this is not the only indication of their power in your program but it is sufficient to demonstrate their significance.

In addition, this committee can be the most helpful component of your expedition team. On the other hand, this committee can stand in your way. How does one choose the members of this committee and what are the best ways to work with them?

The advisory committee and its functions:
One of the requirements of your institution is that you have an advisory committee that is to advise you on your program, monitor your progress, and certify completion of the requirements for degree. For a master's program, this committee may consist of as few as three faculty members, one of whom may be your research advisor. At the other extreme, this committee may consist of six to seven faculty members, again including your research advisor. Typically, the members of this committee will be chosen sometime in your first year in graduate school, but always after the selection of your research advisor (see time lines in section **IV.**). This committee may serve the following **formal** functions.

- To review your past course work and establish your graduate program of study.
- To administer a qualifying examination (see section **XIV.**) For the purpose of assessing your competence in your discipline.
- To advise you and your research advisor on your research program.
- To administer a comprehensive examination (see section **XV**), successful completion of which is required for admission into candidacy for the Ph.D. degree.
- To review your written thesis or dissertation, and to administer an examination which is your defense of the thesis or dissertation.
- To certify that you have successfully completed the requirements for the degree.

- In the case of a master's program, the committee may also recommend for or against your continuation for a Ph.D. degree.

In addition to the formal functions above, this advisory committee is an excellent source of potential mentors for areas that are not covered as well by the research advisor as you might wish (see section **IX.**). **Consult your graduate handbook for all the details relating to the guidance committee members and functions!**

Unfortunately, it is not unusual for a student to be intimidated by the awesome power represented by the advisory committee and to avoid meeting with the committee. In most cases, this is an error in judgment. In the absence of the committee, one person, your research advisor, makes the decisions. The decisions and quality of advice are typically of higher quality when being made by the well-chosen advisory committee. It is never a good idea to wait for an advisory committee meeting until that meeting is forced by some arbitrary bureaucratic deadline. Call a meeting of your committee at *least* once every year. If this is not possible, meet individually with the members of your committee. You want to establish a relationship with these people before they sit in judgment of your work, and a relationship cannot be established if you do not meet with them. Moreover, a working relationship cannot easily be established if every meeting is forced by a deadline.

A meeting of the entire committee at least once a year is also advisable because faculty members in a group may express different "personalities" than when you meet with them individually. Faculty love to talk about research and ideas, and often they can come up with creative ideas together that would not emerge from them individually.

Choosing the members of the advisory committee:
This is a very important committee for you so you need a say in its composition. On the other hand, this is a committee with which your research advisor needs to productively work, so he/she needs a say in its composition. For these reasons, you and your research advisor working together should choose the committee members. Your advisor has a distinct advantage in knowing his/her colleagues, and may have a number of colleagues with whom he/she is accustomed to working. You need to do your homework. Have you taken courses from faculty with whom you felt a good rapport? If so, you should consider them. Do they have an interest which overlaps your research project? This is extremely important. It is not necessary that they be an expert in your research area – it is only necessary that they have an overlapping interest. Talk with students in this person's laboratory or on whose advisory committee this person already serves. Find out what he/she is like. How approachable is he/she? Does he/she maintain appropriate standards? Would he/she be a good mentor? Does this person take the time to talk with advisees? What have the student experiences with him/her been like?

Having done your homework, approach the person and ask for an appointment to discuss the possibility of him/her serving on your advisory committee. Go into that meeting with a copy of your course work for him/her, and be prepared to talk about your background, your career goals, your general research interests, and the specific research project on which you are presently working. Ask questions about his/her interest in this area and his/her willingness to serve on yet another committee, and assess informally for yourself how comfortable it is to have this conversation. Remember, you are going to be working with this person for several years.

After you have talked with a number of potential committee members, review the positives and negatives of each, and make sure that you assess what positive attribute each person is going to bring to the committee. (It might be worthwhile at this point to review the list of mentors you will need from section **IX**). With this information in front of you, sit with your research advisor, and come to a consensus with him/her. Finally, notify the entire committee of the committee composition and schedule your first advisory committee meeting.

IX

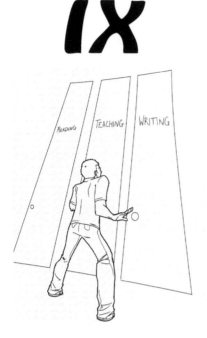

Choosing Mentors for All of the Skills You Will Need in Your Profession

If you were planning an expedition to the summit of Mount Everest, it is unlikely that you would set out without a guide who knew the mountain and those conditions that you would likely encounter. It is unlikely that you would choose as your guide a person who had lived her entire life in the Amazon Valley and had the survival skills necessary for living in the Amazon Jungle but was unfamiliar with Mount Everest. However, if you were planning an expedition in the Amazon Valley, the latter person might be the ideal choice for your guide. We learn to choose a guide, who knows the route we intend to travel, and we learn to change our guides, and have multiple guides, as our journey changes.

The need for a guide is no less necessary to maximize your success in your journey toward your chosen career. We refer to this guide as a mentor. This is named after Mentor, who, in a story from Greek mythology, was requested by his friend Odysseus to be a trusted teacher of Odysseus's son, Telemachus while Odysseus was off for years to the Trojan wars. The choice of mentor or mentors is one of the most important choices of your academic career.

The mentor must be thoroughly knowledgeable about the topic being taught, be willing to teach you, and be capable of passing the necessary information from him/herself to you.

Do not choose a mentor based on one of these attributes. The mentor must be **all** three of the above.

Skills for which you may need mentors:

It is *highly unlikely* that any single individual has the knowledge base with which to guide you in obtaining all of the skills that you need. Imagine yourself as a highly successful professional in your chosen field. What are the skills that you need for this success? The list might include:
- The ability to design and carry out a research project/program.
- The ability to write papers and books describing the results of your research.

64

- The ability to raise the necessary funds to conduct that research.
- The ability to give research lectures or seminars to your colleagues.
- The ability to design a course and teach students.
- The ability to manage a number of people working for you in your research program.
- The ability to use the necessary interpersonal skills to optimize interactions with your administrators, colleagues, and students.
- The ability to enter into a continuing intellectual growth program.
- The ability to balance the necessary roles you have in both your professional and personal life.

You should add to this list the additional skills you see needed for success in your chosen field.

These are some of the skills that you will wish to learn from a mentor. However, perhaps the most common error of the graduate student is the choice of a single mentor from whom they expect to learn all of these skills. Look again at the list above. Can you imagine any single person with the skills to be your mentor in all of these areas? Probably not! Clearly, one needs *multiple* mentors. You have chosen to work on your research with a particular faculty member. This person is thus your research advisor and is your most likely mentor in developing your **research** skills (see section **VI**). As you get to know your research advisor, observe his/her areas of relative strengths and weaknesses.

If your research advisor is relatively weak or even if he/she is not particularly strong in an area that you will need for professional success, then you need to find an additional mentor for that area.

Look first to the members of your advisory committee **(see section VIII)**. If none of the members of your advisory committee have strength in the desired area, then look for the additional mentor outside of your committee. Don't forget to look for mentors outside of the faculty. You should consider staff, other graduate students, post-doctoral associates, etc. The most important element is not their position but their strength in the desired area.

Once you have identified a potential mentor with strengths in the desired area, do some homework. You need to know not only that they have the strengths, but also that they are willing and capable of teaching you in that area. You can get a reasonably good feel for this information by informally chatting with some of the present or past students for whom they have served as a mentor. From such conversations, you can learn how approachable they are, and in fact, how effective they are as a mentor. Finally, approach the potential mentor. Identify the skill that you need to develop, and indicating that they appear to have strengths in this area, ask if they would be willing to serve as your mentor in this arena. Don't ask for a general mentor; ask for a mentor in a specific arena.

Be willing to explicitly discuss your needs and the mentor-student relationship **(see section X)**. Don't take rejection personally. If the response is negative, thank the person for their consideration, and continue your search for a mentor. When accepted, be grateful, and hold up your end of the mentor-student relationship. Continue this process until you have developed the set of mentors you need for professional success. Finally, keep this as an open list. As you develop the need for additional skills in graduate school and beyond, set out to find the mentors you need. Both authors of this book have mentors in a number of areas. This list has constantly changed as our needs have changed.

We are completely serious in our suggestion that you <u>need</u> <u>multiple</u> mentors.

What if your research advisor views him/herself as your sole mentor?

There is one other area in which you need to do some homework. What do you do if your research mentor becomes angry that you have approached other people to be your mentor also? This is a difficult problem and ultimate answers are elusive. However we can explore some possible solutions. First of all, why is this happening? There may be a multitude of reasons, but one seems particularly prevalent. Unfortunately, many faculty members seem to suffer from the mistaken perception that they must appear to be perfect. This includes perfection as an advisor. Their problem becomes your problem if they resent your need for more than one mentor. In essence, your advisor may see your need for additional mentors as a statement of his/her inadequacy. There are some steps you can follow to minimize this potentially abrasive situation.

- A recurrent theme in this book is that your successful completion of a graduate program depends not only on your intelligence, but also on your willingness to learn the political and social skills necessary for success in the academic community. One of the first places these skills will be needed is in the ability to know and work with your advisor. You've done your homework before choosing your advisor. You know from discussions with other students and discussions with your mentor what type of a person he/she is. Will this person encourage you to seek out additional mentors? Will this person be angry if you do so? You should be able to predict the response.

- If your research advisor is an enlightened mentor, he/she will open the topic of skills that you need for success and identify those where you should seek additional mentors. He/she will even have suggestions of likely candidates to serve those needs. If your research advisor is this enlightened, you not only do not have a problem with additional mentors, but also have an excellent mentor from whom you can learn how to be a mentor.

- If your research mentor is not yet enlightened, but appears to be very open to discussion, raise the issue with them over several meetings. For example, in your first meeting, you might ask what skills you will need for success in your professional career. In a future meeting, you might bring in the list you have made of these skills. At some point, you want to lead the discussion to how you should most effectively learn these skills. This is the research advisor's opening to identify those skills on which he/she can effectively mentor you. Either the research advisor or you then needs to raise the remaining issue. How should you learn those remaining skills? If the research advisor plays down the importance of all skills in which they feel they cannot mentor you, and if you truly believe these to be important skills, then you have learned that your research advisor's opinion of his/her duty as a mentor is to turn you into his/her clone. This is not unusual. Remember that your mentor has probably never been taught how to be a mentor. They may perceive that they succeeded in graduate school, and therefore one can succeed by being exactly like them. They have never learned that many different paths can lead to the same destination.

- If it becomes clear that your research advisor will not agree to you choosing additional mentors, you have three options. First, this information about your research advisor may persuade you that you have chosen to work with the

wrong person, and should seek another research advisor who is more open to your professional development needs.
Second, you may choose to stay with this research advisor and give up the idea of additional mentors. Third, you may choose to stay with this research advisor and seek additional mentors surreptitiously. Accomplishing the third option is easier if your additional mentors are members of your advisory committee and if you don't refer to them as mentors. Call them advisors and learn from them; just don't call them mentors.

Be keenly aware that are two persons involved in the mentor-student relationship between you and your mentor. In the next chapter (X), we discuss this relationship in more depth. It is highly unlikely that either you or your mentor is "perfect". It is likely that the most effective mentor is someone you can trust to always give you the truth. Thus, **you** need to be able to hear both positive comments about your activities, and also constructive criticisms for change.

X

*T*he Mentor-Student Relationship

As indicated in section **IX,** above, in planning any serious expedition, you would likely set out with a guide who knew the area to be covered and had the skills for survival. The need for a guide is particularly crucial for your journey toward your chosen career. Perhaps the single most important component of your graduate school experience is the opportunity for you to have one or more mentors.

Your research advisor will be your primary mentor who will guide your journey in research (for more information on the choice of your research advisor, see section **VI**). You may choose other mentors as guides for other skills that you need to develop (for more information on choosing mentors for all of the skills you will need in your profession, see section **IX**). In every relationship between any two people, both parties have an obligation to ensure that the relationship is mutually beneficial. The mentor-student relationship is no exception. Regardless of the skill you wish to develop, if you have a mentor, the mentor will expect some things from you and you will expect some things from the mentor. If both parties work to fulfill these expectations, the relationship will be optimized.

We very strongly suggest that these expectations not be left to chance but rather agreed upon in an open and honest discussion between you and your prospective mentor. The following could serve as the basis for this discussion although both you and your prospective mentor may wish to expand on these items.

Reasonable expectations of the mentor and student:
The mentor has every right to expect that the student is in the program because he/she wants to be, openly displays that interest in the program, and will make every commitment toward completion of the program. The mentor is dedicating time and effort to the student's success. The student must be committed. The mentor likely does not want to donate time and energy to an unwilling or uninvolved student. Similarly, the student has every right to expect that the mentor has the needed knowledge and background required for serving as a mentor in this area. The student has chosen a mentor based largely on the belief that the

prospective mentor is knowledgeable. Whenever the mentor finds that the area is going beyond their knowledge base, they have the obligation to say this to the student.

The mentor has every right to expect that the student will openly appreciate the efforts of the mentor. Being the mentor of a student in a graduate program takes time and effort. Appreciation by the student is some small reward for this investment. Similarly though, the student has every right to expect that the mentor will feel that they succeed as the student succeeds.

The mentor has every right to expect that the student will take responsibility for scheduling regular meetings and will be prompt for those meetings. The student has every right to expect that the mentor will structure advisory meeting in such a way that ideas are easily exchanged. Note that the mentor is given the responsibility for organizing the meeting while the student is given the responsibility for scheduling the meeting. As discussed in section **V.,** the student has a responsibility to always be prompt. The mentor shares this responsibility. The scheduled meeting should begin promptly and not drag out indefinitely.

The mentor has every right to expect that the student will be absolutely honest. This is not the time for "mind games". Honesty and openness are reasonably to be expected. The student has every right to expect that the mentor will be ***constructively*** critical. No person thrives when constantly criticized, or when the criticism tears them down rather than providing them with a path for improvement.

The mentor has every right to expect that the student will give serious consideration to any advice from the mentor whether that advice be positive or negative. The mentor likely does not want to feel that their advice is largely wasted. The student has every right to expect that the mentor will guide and oversee the student's progress. No student wants to waste valuable time with a mentor who is not willing to make the investments of time and effort into being a good mentor.

The mentor has every right to expect that the student will willingly bring any difficulties encountered to the mentor for open discussion. It is typically very difficult to solve problems if they are permitted to reach crisis level. They are far more easily solved before they reach that level. The student has every right to expect that the mentor will be available when needed. In case of a crisis or emergency, no student deserves to be told to wait for their regularly scheduled meeting.

The mentor has every right to expect that the student will take responsibility for producing research and written work that is of high quality. Half way is simply not sufficient in a graduate program. The student has every right to expect that the mentor will be friendly, open, and supportive. The student expects a guide or coach, not a judge and jury.

The mentor has every right to expect that the student will take responsibility for being independent and self-motivated. In the authors' experiences, it has not been possible to install a starter in any student. Other attributes can be taught and encouraged, but the student must be a self-starter. In a similar vein though, the student has every right to expect that the mentor will read the student's work before the scheduled meetings. No student wants to generate work in a timely manner for a scheduled meeting only to find that the mentor did not take the time to read that work.

Are these expectations complete? No! They should be considered as a beginning. Spend some time thinking through each item in the above paragraphs. Particularly think about the relative ease or difficulty of each item. Then, use these items as the basis for the first student-mentor meeting to discuss the expectations of each. Finally, if either the mentor or the student is dissatisfied with the relationship, it should be mutually terminated. **This relationship is the greatest potential benefit of graduate school.** Enjoy it!

For further information, see: Phillips, E. S. and D. S. Pugh. 2000. *How to get a PhD: a handbook for students and their supervisors.* Buckingham [England]: Open University Press.

XI

PASSPORT

Cross-Cultural Communication

We all have the choice of either staying in the relatively small world into which we were born, and in which we were raised, or expanding ourselves for the large world around us. In many cases, our opportunity to expand our world is greatest in graduate school. It is here, in graduate school, that we are most likely to be surrounded by a great diversity of people with many belief systems. More importantly, it is here, in graduate school, that we are surrounded by a large number of people who are truly interested in expanding *themselves* intellectually. It is much easier to grow when you are in an environment where growth is normal, where growth is valued.

Graduate school is a wonderful opportunity to learn about the larger world by learning about the people around you. This is accomplished most effectively through the use of some of the strategies of the cultural anthropologist. The cultural anthropologist studies another culture by living in or around that culture and observing the members of that culture. The observer then tries to define that culture as neutrally as possible. The observer may find that some aspects of the culture are desirable and wish to adopt them.

The observer also may find that some aspects of the culture are undesirable and wish to avoid them. Regardless of the observer's personal judgment of the culture, the goal is to define the culture without bias. In addition, the observer tries to maintain his/her own presence in the culture as neutral as possible. That is, the observer tries not to change the culture being observed. (e.g., remember the admonition often stated on the television series "Star Trek" that the crew must not alter the culture being visited). Moreover, the observer tries not to offend the members of the culture being observed, or to be offended by the members of the culture.

Each of us is a member of many sub-cultures. For example, a person might belong to one sub-culture in their religion, another sub-culture as an academician, yet another sub-culture on their softball team, etc. Each of these sub-cultures has its own set of acceptable behavior, dress, discussion topics, exclusiveness, etc. There may be little if any overlap in the people who belong to these sub-cultures, or alternatively, there may be a great deal of overlap in membership. Belonging to any one of the sub-cultures does not define who you are. However, if the observer knows the sub-cultures to which you belong, that observer has progressed toward an understanding of you, the person.

You have the opportunity in graduate school to become acquainted with a large number of sub-cultures through your observations of and interactions with a great number of diverse people. As you expand the number of the cultures with which you are acquainted, and possibly expand those with which you are comfortable, the size of your world will grow. In addition to expanding your world, there is a very practical reason for studying other cultures. You will be a graduate student in a department that has a particular sub-culture. You are working to become a member of a profession that has a particular sub-culture. The more quickly you can identify the characteristics of a specific sub-culture, the more rapidly you will be capable of taking on the characteristics of that sub-culture, and thus becoming an insider. How can this be achieved? How can you, an outsider, sufficiently observe a sub-culture to know how to become an insider? What a wonderful challenge!

Know your own sub-culture(s):
Imagine being an alien from another solar system and being charged with describing the behavior(s) of earthlings. First, you must know yourself. What are the sub-cultures with which you feel comfortable? Make a list if possible. Now, next to each sub-culture, designate those behaviors that you take on when with others from that sub-culture. How would you recognize the un-informed alien in your midst? These elements that permit the recognition of the un-informed "alien" are the elements that distinguish the insiders from the outsiders. For example, the person who shows up for a game of pick-up basketball wearing a suit is likely an outsider. This does not mean that an "alien" might not become an accepted and valuable member of that sub-culture at some time. It does mean that it is evident that the outsider is an "alien", and that acceptance may have to be "earned".

Read non-verbal communication:
Much of our communication is not verbal. Much of the message is in the tone of voice or particularly in the facial expressions, hand signs, interpersonal distance, and other movements that constitute our non-verbal communication. We all learn as very young children to read non-verbal communication. Perhaps in its simplest case, we easily distinguish a frown from a smile. As we grow, the sophistication of our non-verbal communication grows along with the sophistication of our verbal language.

Have you ever watched the teacher who "teaches" to his/her notes or book, never looking at the students? Remember how disconnected that teacher was? Why? He/she presented the material rather than teaching the students. He/she refused to read your "non-verbal communication". As you are watching other people's non-verbal communication, you will see a number of people who quite consciously use a "poker face". They reduce the amount of information that they offer by reducing the non-verbal communication. The "poker face" in itself is non-verbal communication, and can give you a great deal of information about the person's comfort level with others.

Observe the sub-culture around you:
Through observation, try to determine the answers to the following questions:
- Is there a "typical" greeting?
- Is there a clothing convention?
- Are there particular conversation topics that are preferred?
- What is the accepted style of inter-personal non-verbal communication? This may be different for the same power level, for a top-down power differential, for a bottom-up power differential, for a cross-gender encounter.

- What are the traits that appear to have contributed to the success of an advanced student who appears to be held in high regard in the department?

Answering these questions will give you a start on your characterization of the professional sub-culture in which you wish to be accepted. Now, as you observe the behavior of others in your university, and others outside your university but within your chosen profession, you can begin to distinguish between those aspects of the culture that are specific to your mentor/department/institution, and those that are general for academia or your chosen field. This process outlined above is exactly what you would do if you visited another country and it is that same skill that you can apply in any new situation such as a new graduate program.

Which aspects of the sub-culture are general and which are specific?

Once you have identified the traits that appear to be held by successful people in your department, in academia or in your chosen field, you will be faced with a series of decisions that may be difficult. Which of these traits should you consider emulating? If any of these traits is so repulsive to you that you cannot imagine adopting the trait while being true to yourself, then you should reject that trait. However, if that trait appears to be absolutely required for success, then you may wish to re-consider your professional career decisions. Keep in mind that you are already a member of a number of sub-cultures, and that you change your behavior to match the particular sub-culture with which you are presently interacting. It then follows that you may not need to radically alter your personality to be an insider in an additional sub-culture. You will find though that inclusion is made easier by adopting the necessary behaviors to match that particular sub-culture while you are interacting with its members. If you choose to adopt behaviors to match the sub-culture, don't reject the person who chooses not to do so. Similarly, if you choose not to adopt behaviors to match the sub-culture, don't reject the person who does so.

Don't offend!
Remember the caution we raised at the beginning of this section. It is extremely easy in any cross-cultural communication to offend or to be offended. In most cases, the offense is not intentional, but happens out of ignorance. You wish to decrease the probability of offending others first because it's simply not productive, but also because it may get in the way of your personal progress. To minimize offense to others there is really one rule: treat others with respect. However, respect is seldom identical across cultures, across genders, and across age groups. Some cautionary notes follow which can guide you:

- Treat other people with the same respect you feel is due to your mother, grandmother, or another person you hold in particularly high esteem.
- Avoid making personal comments about others. You can demonstrate your interest in the person without making comments about that person to others.
- Treat other peoples' offices, homes and laboratories with respect. **Never** browse through or read anything on another person's desk. **Never** re-arrange their office, laboratory or home unless invited. For example, let us say that your research advisor has invited you to his/her home for dinner. Assume that they have planned the evening. They have chosen the music, food, entertainment, *etc.* as they wish to entertain. This is your opportunity to observe behavior in their sub-culture. Don't impose your own. To do so would make the very loud and

rather arrogant statement that you find their sub-culture to be inferior or intolerable.

- If you are asked about your sub-culture, be willing to share that information. This indicates respect of you and your sub-culture by the one asking the question, and indicates that you respect them when you are willing to share.

- When you see evidence of a cultural difference, accept that difference simply as a difference. **Never** get involved in a discussion of better and worse with respect to cultural differences.

Have fun!

This is one of the most wonderful aspects of graduate school. You can share ideas and cultural behaviors with others, permitting the world of all involved to grow. Daryl Davis, author of *Klan-destine relationships: a black man's odyssey in the Ku Klux Klan* (New Horizon Press; Far Hills, NJ. 1998; 315 pp.), points out that whenever he "actively seeks to learn about someone else, he passively teaches them about himself." Please re-read this paragraph. There is a great deal of wisdom in Daryl Davis' approach.

XII

Your Physical Environment

So, you have decided to go from Puerto Rico to Minnesota or from Maine to Southern California for graduate school. This is a significant transition, not just in the intellectual demands, or in the level of cultural diversity, but also in your physical environment. The largest single error that you can make is to totally avoid that new environment, and to retreat into your office, the library, and your apartment. Is it totally different? Is it intimidating? Is it somewhat dangerous or frightening? Yes, probably, but this is not an adequate reason for retreat. The person who insists that his/her home environment is the "best in the world" has bored us all. This person makes themselves and those around them miserable by actively missing home. To avoid this trap, follow two steps. First, **learn** about your new environment. Second, **actively embrace** that environment.

Learn about your new environment:

In any environment, there are some components that can be dangerous for the uninitiated, but are not regarded as dangerous by the native. For instance, the ocean, desert, mountain, jungle, city, country, extreme cold or extreme heat all can be dangerous for the uninformed. The solution is obvious. Inform yourself. Find travel guides, or a willing and informed native, and learn about your new physical environment.

Learn about the opportunities in sports, arts, outdoor activities, *etc.* for your new environment. Don't dismiss them out of hand because they are different from that to which you have grown accustomed. For example, some opportunities available in the Middle West may not be available in the southwestern desert. However, other opportunities specific to the new environment are available. One has to learn to carry adequate water, and to dress appropriately for the climate, for example. Once a few relatively simple rules are learned, the desert becomes a wonderful place for exploration. In no part of the country is there a lack of potential dangers, but in no part of the country is there a lack of potential for exploration and excitement.

Actively embrace your new environment:

Once you've learned about your new environment, actively explore it. Try out new activities and replace old habits with new. For example, if you find yourself in the far north, don't hide from the winter. Learn about the appropriate ways to dress in cold weather, and then go out and revel in the winter. Learn to ski, go camping in the snow, and make "snow angels." By embracing the new environment, you will maintain a positive attitude toward your environment and yourself. This positive attitude is one of the most important components for getting you through graduate school, and the positive attitude will still be there long after graduate school is over.

XIII

Personal Safety

The power differentials in graduate school:
In graduate school, there is inevitably a great difference in power
between you, the graduate student, and many of the people around
you. For example, you will work very closely with your research
advisor, and to a great extent, your professional career is balanced
on the relationship between the two of you. Thus, your research
advisor may be seen as having a great deal of power over you. On
the other hand, you will likely be a teaching assistant for one or

more classes. In this case, you may be seen as having a great deal of power over your students who may be approximately the same age as you or perhaps only slightly younger.

Whenever there is a power differential, there is the potential for misuse of that power. Increasingly, universities and graduate schools are aware of this potential for misuse of power and, in many cases, have instituted rules or guidelines to decrease the probability of that misuse. These misuses of power are generally as follows:

- Inappropriate assignment of duties.
- Verbal/ psychological abuse.
- Physical/sexual interactions.

In this section, we will talk about the potential for you to be a victim, or for you to victimize someone else. We will also talk about ways to avoid these traps, and where to go for assistance if the need arises.

Don't be a victim - don't be a predator!

Although the great majority of mentor-student relationships are both productive and appropriate, in some situations, the student may become a victim. The research advisor may serve as mentor, judge, and close friend. It is the responsibility of the research advisor to maintain this as an appropriate relationship. The advisor must carefully avoid abuse of the student either in workload or assignment of duties, in psychological/emotional interactions, in verbal diatribes, or in any physical/sexual interactions. Similarly, the student must be aware of the possibilities for abuse, and recognize such situations as inappropriate before they progress too far. For example, if the student is receiving financial assistance from the institution in the form of a fellowship which carries no requisite duties, or financial assistance from the department for being a teaching assistant in a particular course, it is totally inappropriate for the research advisor to assign duties unrelated to those for which the stipend was intended.

For example, under these circumstances, it would be inappropriate for the student to be requested to type a manuscript, or provide child care for the advisor's children "as part of the student's duties for support." In a case such as this, the student might indicate to the advisor that they were under the impression that the stipend did not include such duties. If the advisor persisted, the next avenues of approach would be the department ombudsperson or possibly chairperson, or the graduate school ombudsperson or dean. It is best that such matters be worked out informally. Once such a problem becomes formal, it may be difficult to maintain a cordial working relationship with the advisor, so an alternate arrangement may need to be constructed.

Constructive criticism is a necessary component of every mentor-student relationship. However, it is conceivable that your advisor will critique you or your work in ways that you may perceive as showing disrespect for you as a person. For example, you might be berated in public, or called stupid. These are inappropriate behaviors. If such behavior is blatant or persistent, you should sit with your advisor and indicate how you feel as a consequence of that behavior. Remember that your first objective is to educate the person and is based on the first assumption that the behavior is the consequence of ignorance. If this encounter is negative or if the behavior persists, the next avenues of approach are the department and then graduate school ombudspersons. You should also take the opportunity to obtain information from your graduate school on conflict resolution (see section **XVIII**).

Verbal disrespect is one of the most difficult types of inappropriate behavior to assess. So many people routinely show verbal disrespect for others that many of us give permission for others to verbally victimize us by not confronting such situations. The bottom line is that graduate school is a place in which you should be strongly encouraged to grow intellectually. No one should stay in an academic situation in which his/her involvement feels personal and not professional. Note that you also have a responsibility not to inflict verbal abuse on any of your students. The encouragement of intellectual growth cannot effectively happen in an abusive environment.

We are all sexual beings. However, it is increasingly recognized in academia that <u>any</u> sexual contact should be prohibited between two individuals one of whom has power over the other. Any non-consensual sexual contact is clearly forbidden. Consensual contact is typically strongly discouraged. Being "in love" is wonderful. However, experience teaches us that the path of relationships is seldom free of conflict. Breaking up can be horrible. Breaking up when there is a power differential can be a devastating experience.

In particular, the trust necessary for an effective mentor-student relationship is damaged and can be destroyed. For this reason, even consensual contact is ill advised and typically strongly discouraged or forbidden. Although not all situations can be covered by simple rules, the following generalization will cover most situations. **Have no sexual/romantic involvement either with anyone who holds power over you, or with anyone over whom you hold power.** Violations of the prohibitions against sexual contact should be pursued through the legal system and through your graduate school and university. It should be evident from this discussion that this is an extremely sensitive but serious area. Because of this, it is only good sense to avoid even the appearance of flirting with anyone over you, or under you.

Where to go for help:
Possible places to go for help and/or support include:
- Department ombudsperson.
- Department chairperson.
- Graduate school ombudsperson or dean.
- University ombudsperson.
- Women's resource center.
- Campus police.
- Community police.
- Community Resource Center.

Remember that the great majority of mentor-student relationships are healthy and productive. Know the limits of appropriate behavior, and work very hard to keep yourself from being <u>neither</u> a victim <u>nor</u> a predator.

We strongly recommend that everyone read the following book by Gavin DeBecker. Although targeted toward women, the points that he makes are equally valid for both women and men.

De Becker, G.. 1998. *The gift of fear: Survival signals that protect us from violence.* Dell Publishing.

XIV

*A*dditional Resources
of Your University

You are not only going to school. You are becoming a member of
an academic community and that community has many resources
that are available for you. However, their effective use will require
initiative on your part. The following resources are likely
available.

- **Computer facilities.** Where is the computer center? Does
  the University provide access to the Internet? Do you have
  access to computers in your department?

- **Counseling center.** Life is not without stress, and graduate school may add a number of stresses. Most educational institutions provide access to mental health facilities at low or no cost for students.
- **Cultural centers.** Most educational institutions support a number of cultural activities. As a student, you may be eligible for tickets for events at reduced prices.
- **Support office for students with disabilities.** Many students have disabilities and most campuses have an office to assist those students toward full participation in campus life.
- **Family resources.** Many graduate students have their own families, and many institutions provide access to graduate student family housing, childcare centers, etc.
- **Graduate School.** View the graduate school as a resource for information, programs, potential funding, and assistance in conflict resolution.
- **Health services.** Most campuses have a separate center which provides access to physical health services at low cost for students.
- **Housing.** Most educational institutions have at least some housing for graduate students. This housing is typically more convenient than off-campus housing, and frequently is less expensive.
- **Learning center.** This center may provide information and counseling on testing items such as the GRE, and assistance with learning difficulties. There also may be assistance on developing writing skills.
- **Library.** Do not underestimate the value of this resource. Access to computers has not made the library obsolete. Seek out a tour of the library. Explore the library and its services. You will need these later, and typically, when you need the library, you're facing a deadline. Explore it now.

- **Minority Affairs (Diversity) Offices.** These offices may provide literature, information, counseling, and access to minority interest groups.
- **Public safety.** Many campuses maintain their own department of public safety. Don't wait for a crisis to find out how to make contact with public safety. Inform yourself about parking regulations *before* you get a parking ticket.
- **Recreation.** Don't neglect your physical self while you are training your mental self. Maintain your body through regular exercise either through team or individual sports. Most campuses have recreation facilities for use by students.
- **Religious groups.** A number of churches, mosques, temples and synagogues will be found in your community. Remember that you are an academic person but that you are much, much more.
- **Seminars and lectures.** Most university departments offer many seminars and lectures. These provide wonderful opportunities to hear presentations by renowned speakers. There are also opportunities to broaden yourself by attending lectures and seminars in areas outside of your own.
- **Support staff.** The support staff of the department is the glue that holds the unit together and the lubricant to keep it moving. Members of the support staff are seldom in the limelight. They typically don't win advanced degrees or bring in large amounts of money. However, without the support staff, the unit will very quickly cease to operate. Treat the people in the support staff with respect and dignity. They deserve it, and they can make your time in the unit far easier.
- **Women's Resource Center.** This center may provide literature, counseling, and a safe-place when needed.

XV

*T*he Qualifying Examination

Many departments will have a qualifying examination. To cross this hurdle, you must demonstrate competence in the subject matter covered by that department. This examination is typically administered to students at the end of their first year of graduate school, and must be successfully passed before the student can establish an official program of graduate study. The general philosophy of such an exam is that you will eventually display an advanced degree from that department and institution, so you should possess the minimal knowledge of subject matter considered to be important in that field. Thus, the assumption is that your bachelor's degree is not sufficient evidence of that knowledge base, but an adequate performance on an examination administered by the graduate department is sufficient evidence of your knowledge base.

To prepare yourself for the qualifying examination, depend heavily on your mentors and other students. Find out who writes the examination, who grades the examination, and what areas are covered by the examination. Then, study the areas covered *as though you were studying for a final examination in a course*. In addition, find out what sort of questions have previously been asked, and what things are considered important by the person(s) writing the questions. This may guide your study. Study together with other students. Perhaps the best test for your knowledge base is your ability to explain a topic to someone else. Test each other thoroughly. Don't underestimate the amount of time required to study for a qualifying examination. How many areas does it cover? You must be adequately prepared in all areas. Don't "cram" for the qualifying examination, eat well, arrive early, and don't walk into the examination in a sleep-deprived state.

For each question on the qualifying examination, follow several steps in sequence. First, read the question. Second, think about the question. Third, think through the answer to the question. Fourth, only after the first three steps have been completed, pick up your pen or pencil (or put your fingers onto the keyboard) and answer the question. This sequence is *very* important. We get into the habit of rapidly writing answers to questions, and this can be dangerous if we have not adequately understood the question, or if we have been exercising our hand, writing potentially incorrect sentences, while we are thinking through the correct answer. In summary, be rested, be alert, be prepared, and be cautious. You have progressed this far because of your competence; ***don't*** be arrogant, but ***do*** be confident.

XVI

Comprehensive Examination

As you saw in the time line in section **IV**, at the beginning of your Ph.D. degree, you are involved mostly in taking course work. You may then become increasingly involved over the next two years in research. Sometime around the end of your second year or possibly your third year, when you have completed most of your course work, you will take the comprehensive examination. Typically, your institution will define that this is to be completed at a particular time (this may range from the end of your first year to the end of your third year), and following the completion of a particular percentage of your courses (e.g., 80%). Successful completion of this examination is required before you can proceed with your degree, so this is one of your major hurdles.

Who administers the examination?

The comprehensive examination may be administered by your department or by your advisory committee. If administered by your department, a single, written examination may be given to all students at that level in the department that year, or there may be a department-designated committee that specifically examines you. If the exam is administered by your department, you need to determine from the department the areas, and the timing, length, etc. of the examination. From your fellow graduate students who have previously completed the exam, find out what the exam is like. If your advisory committee administers the exam, you will need to determine this information from the members of your advisory committee.

What might a typical comprehensive examination look like?

Remember that there may be considerable variation in the nature of a comprehensive exam. However, the following is a common format. In this format, the members of the advisory committee decide on areas in which you will be examined. At a particular, pre-selected date, you will begin the exam. On each day, or possibly every other day, you will take an exam written by one member of your committee. This is continued until you have completed the written component from each committee member. Typically, one to two weeks later, you get together with the committee members for the oral examination, which may take 2-4 hours. At the end of the oral exam, the committee makes a joint assessment of your performance. Let's look at these various steps, and talk about ways to optimize your performance.

Studying:

First, you want to determine the appropriate subject areas for study. Each committee member has indicated the area in which he/she will exam you. Approximately **six months** before the exam, talk with each committee member and ask for guidance in preparing for his/her section of the exam. If you have had a course from that person, he/she may indicate that you should review that course. He/she may suggest particular literature for you to study. Take these suggestions seriously. If a committee member has suggested that you read a particular set of papers, do not ignore the suggestion for any reason.

Once you have determined what to study, set up a schedule for yourself with a time block set aside each day leaving approximately **three months** to prepare yourself for the examination. If you find that you are most alert in the early morning, then study in the morning. If you're more alert in the evening, study in the evening. Schedule rewards for yourself. Make certain that you permit yourself time **each** day for something that is enjoyable for you.

This can be a very intense time, and many students find that engaging in physical exercise each day in addition to the mental exercise of exam preparation better preserves their mental health. Don't delude yourself! You do not have time to ignore either your physical or mental health. Don't panic! You will not learn everything. You do want to maximize the depth of your knowledge in each area. You may find it best to study one area until finished, and then begin a second area. On the other hand, you may find it best to study all or several of the areas each day. Experiment with different approaches to determine what works best for you.

During this study time, when you're taking breaks, talk with the students who work with these committee members, and with students who have taken exams from these committee members. Find out what their questions look like. Do they typically look for facts, theory, thought, etc?

In addition, find out what these committee members are interested in at the moment. If you have a committee member who is presently excited about and working on a particular topic, it is highly likely that you will get a question about that topic.

Attend departmental seminars! Frequently, the seminar will outline a topic that is considered "hot" in your field. As such, the seminars will be excellent sources for questions.

Do **not** attempt to cram for your comprehensive exam. The exam is too extensive. The cramming strategy simply won't work. You want the information in your "long-term memory", not your "short –term" memory. There is simply too much information to have it solely in "short-term memory".

The examination process:

The written portion of the comprehensive examination:
You've completed your studying and the time has come for your first written exam. Make certain that you're taking the exam in a quiet, comfortable place, and follow one major rule - **maintain a positive attitude!** Read through all of the questions. Before you begin to answer any question, think and make notes to organize your answer. After you have mentally organized your answer, then begin to write the answer itself.

We have all watched the teacher or other academic who appears not to know the answer to a question so re-phrases the question into another second frequently-unrelated question and then answers the second question. This is a dangerous strategy to use on your comprehensive exam.

Your examiners are bright; they are not likely to be fooled by this strategy. Answer the question asked; try to avoid the temptation to write about something else that you happen to know better. After you have completed the exam, review it and make notes for yourself about what you feel that you knew and what you wish that you had known more about. Get a good night's sleep, and proceed with the next exam.

After you've completed your written examinations, contact each committee member and ask if there are areas that you should emphasize in your preparation for the oral examination. You already know those areas that you knew inadequately, so prepare yourself in those areas. ***Don't make the same mistakes twice.***

The oral portion of the comprehensive examination:
Approach the oral examination as your first formal opportunity to have an intellectual and academic discussion with those people, your committee members, who will soon be your academic colleagues.

In a typical format, each committee member will ask you questions for a half hour or so and then pass to the next committee member. This continues until there are no further questions. The questioning will usually begin with the opportunity for you to clarify or correct an answer from your written examination that was incorrect or shallow. The questions will frequently proceed into a new area from there.
Some oral comprehensive exams also include a segment in which you defend your dissertation research proposal. Consult the graduate handbook in your program for the pertinent details.

When a question is being asked, listen carefully to the **entire question**! Don't begin to answer until the complete question has been asked. If you do not understand the question, ask that it be restated. Take the time to think about your answer before beginning to talk. If you or the committee is uncomfortable with the brief silence, indicate that you are thinking through the question and its answer.

Don't try to "con" the questioner or "B.S." your way through the answer. If you don't know, **say** that you don't know, but can take a guess, and then, to the best of your ability, base that guess on the pieces of information that you do recall. That way, the answer is seen as a best guess, and not an attempt to "sell" misinformation.

Typically, in the oral exam, the student is not being asked to spit back facts. Are there exceptions? Of course there are. However, you have done your homework, and you know whether or not you have a committee member who emphasizes factual information. In general there are three types of questions:

The first is intended to determine whether or not you, the student, know the information.
The second is intended to demonstrate that the person asking the question knows the information.
The third is the question you really want. This is the question to obtain information that the questioner does not already have. In all three cases, treat every question seriously, and give it your best answer.

Typically, in the oral exam, the emphasis is on the integration of knowledge. Can you use the information you have at your disposal from several different areas to respond to a new area of questioning?

104

Maintain your poise! There is no area of information about which you know everything. On the other hand, there are probably few, if any, areas about which you know nothing. The task for your committee members is to try to assess your **depth** of knowledge in the particular area. For this reason, the questioning on a particular topic will typically continue until you have reached the limit of your knowledge. Be prepared for this. It can be depressing for the questions to continue on a topic until you don't know, and then go to a different topic. Once you are finished with the answer to a particular question, stop talking. Don't ramble on and on. Not only is this clumsy, but you have a high probability of saying something that is incorrect during your rambling.

The results:
When the desire of your committee to ask questions has been exhausted, you will be excused and they will discuss your performance. Following that discussion, you will be invited to return, and they will give you their collective assessment. They have a number of options. In the best of all possible worlds, you will receive a clear "pass," and congratulations are in order. In the worst case, you may be told that your performance was inadequate, and that you may repeat the exam in another number of months.

Typically, only two attempts are permitted, but this may be different in your institution. Consult your graduate handbook prior to the exam so you know your options. Between the best case and worst case are a number of options. For example, you may have passed for all but one committee member. You may be asked to repeat that single examination. In the questioning, the committee may have found that there is a single, important area which you should know, but you know little, if anything.

In this case, it is common to require that you take an additional course in that area. If you do not receive a clear pass, talk with your committee members and make sure that you understand what is expected of you to remedy any deficiencies.

While the comprehensive examination is a significant hurdle, it should be viewed as your first opportunity to demonstrate the depth of your knowledge and your outstanding qualifications for inclusion in the academic arena. Like a road sign on a toll road, it is most significant before you get to it. After you have passed it, its significance pales, and new hurdles and opportunities present themselves.

XVII

The Thesis or Dissertation

Writing:
In graduate school, you will be asked to do a great deal of writing. This will range from papers for individual courses to proposals, abstracts for conferences, and hopefully, manuscripts for papers and books. Under an ideal mentor, you will be asked to submit sections of your research in writing and will receive back *constructive* critiques so that your writing improves with time. In addition, you should be reading papers in the journals of your field

not only for their content, but so that you can see what style(s) is (are) acceptable, and can evaluate what writing to emulate.

Your advisor should also give you manuscripts and proposals for you to develop your own abilities to constructively critique. By the time you arrive at your thesis or dissertation, you should have a lot of practice with writing. However, you will likely find your thesis or dissertation to be the most difficult writing you have yet undertaken. First, it will probably be the longest item you have yet written. Second, it will need to be approved by your research advisor and advisory committee. Several rules will make this hurdle easier.

- **Allow enough time.** Beyond the research itself, it is extremely rare for the **writing** of a thesis or dissertation to take less than two months. Build in twice this time for the process. The panic that happens when you are staring at a deadline and the writing is proceeding slowly doesn't help. Planning enough time for the process will help reduce that panic.
- **Make an extensive outline.** The very length of the thesis or dissertation can inhibit the process. Spend a period of time early-on writing an extensive outline. Go over the outline with your advisor and make certain that you're working on the project on which **both** of you agree. The more detailed the outline, the better. With a detailed outline, you can pick a single piece out of the outline to work on and successfully accomplish that task within a fairly short time. Thus, you've built in the possibility of short-term success and positive feedback.
- **Set a specific target for each day.** You may well have many competing tasks to accomplish each day. Most students find that it works effectively if they set a target for each day

for two, three or four pages. At the completion of that target, then the remainder of the day is yours to work on the other competing tasks. If the writing is not made into a high priority, it is highly unlikely that it will be done.

- **Reward yourself.** Once you have written your target amount each day, or at the end of a particularly onerous section, reward yourself (movies, exercise, etc). Maintain a healthy positive attitude by giving yourself positive feedback. Be particularly cautious that you not ignore your significant other or children.

- **Don't leave data presentation for last.** If you are in a field that is data-driven and in which data is presented in figures or tables, work on these **before** you work on the written components. Typically, having the figures and tables in front of you will help enormously in their written description.

- **Leave adequate time for editing.** Never assume that you can write final copy on your first draft. Your writing will require extensive editing, and editing takes time.

- **Organize.** You will likely organize the thesis or dissertation in chapters. Establish beforehand when your advisor wants to see the manuscript. Does he/she want to see it in its entirety for the first time, or to see it chapter by chapter? Make life easier for yourself; adhere to this agreement.

- **Accept criticism gracefully.** This is work into which you have invested a large amount of yourself. However, criticism should **not** be taken as criticism of yourself. Criticism should be accepted as one additional learning process designed to improve the quality of the product and to educate you in how to better write for your field. Try to be grateful that the critic has taken the time to suggest ways by which the manuscript can be improved. Getting angry not only won't help, but will severely impede the process. Approach the criticism component as an opportunity for you with the help of your advisor to improve the product.

Approval by the committee:
After the thesis or dissertation draft has been approved by your advisor, it's time to give it to the advisory committee. Talk with your advisor first to make sure he/she agrees that it is time for the committee members to read the draft. Leave them adequate time to read and critique the draft before the scheduled defense. Most institutions have a minimum time period (such as two weeks) between the scheduled defense and the day the committee receives the draft. It simply doesn't pay to pressure your committee into a rushed job. The fact that you have been slow is not a reason for your committee members to hurry. Remember, this is **your** top priority. It is probably **not** your committee's top priority. If for some reason, a committee member is **extremely** slow, request that your advisor intercede on your behalf.

Typically, informal feedback will be given to the advisor by the committee members before the defense. If there are major problems, take the time to iron them out if at all possible before the formal defense.

Seminar:
Usually, a formal, public seminar on your work will precede the defense. This should be well planned, rehearsed, timed correctly, and above all, professional. Practice in front of an audience until you are comfortable with the material, with how to present the material clearly, and with responding to questions. Welcome into this audience more senior students who have experience in presenting seminars. Welcome questions. Questions from your audience demonstrate that others are interested in the topic on which you have labored long and hard.

Defense of the dissertation:
Soon after the seminar, sometime on the same day or shortly thereafter, you will assemble with your advisor and advisory committee to defend the thesis or dissertation. By now, you should be an expert on this topic. However, that does not mean that you know everything.

Approach this defense as an opportunity to have an academic discussion with your senior colleagues on the topic you have been working on for a considerable time. The questions may be designed to determine how much you know. They may be designed to demonstrate that you do not yet know everything. They may be designed to demonstrate the knowledge of the person asking the question. They may be designed to determine how well you can think about something that neither you nor anyone else knows. Take them all in your stride. Take your time, think, respond carefully, and do **not** take the questions personally. Remember that you are or should be the expert on your dissertation topic! This does **not** mean that you know everything. On the other hand, neither do your examiners.

After all of your committee members have had adequate time to question you, you will be excused and they will discuss your performance. As was the case with the comprehensive examination, they may choose to give you a clear pass, they may request substantially more work, or they may give you a pass conditional upon re-writing sections of the thesis or dissertation.

Once final approval of the thesis or dissertation has been obtained, this will be indicated by signatures on yet one more administrative action form. This form, and the clean, edited thesis or dissertation, is then taken over one last hurdle.

111

Approval by the Graduate School:
There is typically one last hurdle. This is the approval of the style of the thesis or dissertation by a person (usually in the graduate school) representing the institution. This person will make certain that the copy is on the correct weight of paper, that the margins are the designated size etc. Make your life easier. Find out ahead of time what the requirements are and **adhere to them to the letter**. Be pleasant with this person. They do not make the rules. If you inform yourself as to the requirements and follow those requirements, both your life and the life of the person in the Graduate School will be smoother.

In summary, the writing of a thesis or dissertation can be extremely difficult. However, if you know what to do and organize yourself properly to get it done, this process will go smoothly and congratulations will soon be in order.

*T*he Management and Resolution of Conflicts

(This chapter has been written with the assistance of Dr. Karen Klomparens, Dean of the Graduate School of Michigan State University)

Just as in everyday life, you will encounter conflicts in your graduate program. However, not all conflicts are to be avoided.

Intellectual Conflict

Conflicts may arise over the nature of ideas and theories, about the meaning and interpretation of data gathered in an experiment, and other intellectual activities. These are all part of the academic life. Part of your graduate school experience will be to learn how to critically think about the ideas of others and to put forth and defend your own ideas. Conflicts of this nature are to be expected. These conflicts should not be resolved but should be managed. That is, these conflicts should be intellectual, not personal. Don't avoid intellectual conflicts but don't take them personally.

Conflicts can also arise from other interactions. Conflicts over unspoken expectations that are not met, over the "unwritten" rules in a particular discipline (e.g., the politics of the discipline), or over deeply held personal values are often much more personal and more difficult to manage and resolve. Conflicts of this second type may be defined as interpersonal conflicts. They may also arise out of an intellectual conflict that is permitted to become personal.

Interpersonal Conflicts

One way to avoid interpersonal conflicts is to be sure that you have communicated, and truly listened, to faculty, especially your advisor, about expectations. Good communication can help you avoid many difficulties. What are your expectations? What are the expectations of your advisor, major professor, department, and graduate student colleagues? Clarify misunderstandings. Find out about the unwritten rules by following the advice in Sections **V** and **XI** on politics in the academic institution. Consult your graduate handbook and/or university graduate manuals for specific expectations of students early in your program and use the information you gather from these sources whenever possible to help you avoid unnecessary conflicts.

If you do find yourself in an interpersonal conflict with another student or with a faculty member, here are some tips for resolving the conflict:

- Keep in mind that your primary goal is to obtain your degree. It can be risky to challenge the decisions or opinions of some faculty members. However, ignoring the problem often makes it worse.
- Identify your underlying interests and values within the context of the conflict. If you have stated a position about what you want, think about *why* this is important to you. The other person should do the same. Talking about your interests rather than your positions provides an opportunity to come up with more creative options in order to resolve the conflict.
- Learn to accept constructive criticism. If you are not receiving input on your work, ask for it (see section **X**).
- Make sure that you have checked the department graduate handbook to see if there are any policies that cover your situation. You may also want to look at the University policies that cover graduate education.
- Timeliness is important. If you wait too long, you may not be able to appeal a decision about a grade, for example. Knowing the university or department policy can help you avoid a delay that could cost you your right to an appeal. On the other hand, it is rarely wise to file an official appeal on the same day as the alleged offense. Cool down! Then respond!
- Document everything. People forget. Sometimes you can avoid conflict simply by having important agreements on paper and reminding faculty and others about their promises.
- Make sure that you have the facts on the issue. Gossip and rumors abound at universities; don't fall for them.

- Maintain a problem-solving attitude. Getting angry or burning bridges never pays off. Personal attacks cause more problems than they solve.
- Ask for help if you need advice, a sounding board or a mediator. Most campuses have an Ombudsperson Office, mediation facilities, or personnel in departments or the graduate school who can help you sort out issues.
- Always try to resolve the conflict informally before you use the formal grievance procedure.
- Avoid revenge! There is an old Chinese proverb that says: "if you seek revenge, you had better dig two graves," meaning that you'll do yourself in also. Work in good faith to resolve the conflict.
- This last tip is a repeat of the first tip. Keep in mind that your primary goal is to obtain your degree.

Suggested reading: Roger Fisher, William Ury. 1991. *Getting to yes: negotiating agreement without giving in.* 2nd edition. Penguin Books. New York.

XIX

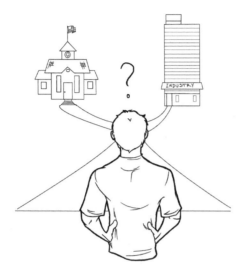

What if You Don't Succeed?

So, let us imagine that your worst nightmare has just come true.
Your graduate dean, research advisor, department chair, *etc.* has
just indicated to you that you have not met the minimum
requirements to continue working in your graduate program. What
now? This section is designed to lead you through a number of
possible steps. It is hoped that you will not face this situation, but
if you do need this section, it is important that you put into place a
number of mechanisms designed so that you: maintain your pride

in yourself; learn from the experience; explore your possible options; and land on your feet.

Perhaps the most important thing for most of us to remember is that our career is *not* identical with our life. We frequently tend to identify ourselves with our career, but we are far more than this. Think of all of the things that you may be (scientist, student, teacher, parent, friend, writer, wood worker, gardener, etc.) Don't limit yourself by defining yourself as your career. (For a humorous book with this point, read "Half asleep in frog pajamas" by Tom Robbins; Bantam Books, New York, 1994, 386 pp.).

Is this a final decision?
At some level, you may well have seen this coming, but you might also be completely surprised by the decision. The first question to ask is whether or not the decision is final. Is there an additional hurdle that would restore your position in the graduate program? If so, find out all of the details. Can the decision be appealed? If so, what is the appeal process? If the decision is not final, *rationally* explore the steps that are available to you.

Anger and frustration, however accurately they may describe your true feelings, have no place in this discussion. Maintain control, obtain information, and be polite. Remember that *you may need help tomorrow from the person you confront today.* If the decision *is* final, this is not a permit for expression of your feelings.

Demonstrate by the very way in which you accept the decision that you have the maturity to be in the graduate program. Moreover, if the decision is indeed final, a temper tantrum is useless. Accept the decision with as much grace as you can muster, and proceed to the next steps.

Learn from the experience:
Throughout life, most personal growth comes through adversity. No, you weren't really in the mood to build more character. However, seldom is the path in this journey defined by our mood. It is now character-building time, so let's get on with and through it.

First of all *do not panic!* This is *not* the end of the world. Your life will *not* become suddenly unraveled tomorrow morning. *Do not panic!* Take a bit of time to think productively about your experience in the graduate program. Be honest with yourself! Why have you not succeeded? Which of the reasons can be attributed directly to you? Which of the reasons can be attributed to the system?

- What are your traits *etc.* that resulted in your leaving the graduate program? Don't be satisfied with casual answers. Insist that you give yourself in-depth answers. For example, perhaps you were unable to maintain your grade point average above the minimum for the institution. That is an answer, but not in sufficient depth. **Why** was your GPA below the minimum? **Why** did you not perform better in your course work? Was your background adequate? Did you study enough? Did you turn materials in on time? For yourself, determine *exactly* what happened. Be careful; it is probably not a single factor. Likely, several things contributed to your lack of success.
- What were the characteristics of the system that contributed to your leaving the graduate program? Again, be honest! Did you have to work outside to support yourself and have inadequate time left for your classes? Did your mentor(s) give you poor advice? Did you feel that your peers excluded you, and that you therefore missed out on important study opportunities with your peers?

Knowing *what* happened; now work to convert that into a learning experience. Of all of the things that happened, could you have done anything differently that would have changed the end result? To what extent were you impacted by the system? Can any of these lessons be incorporated into life style changes to prevent problems in the future?

Incorporate your lessons into a letter to the Dean of the Graduate School. Spell out why you were not successful, including your own problems and those of the system. Do you have to write this letter? No! You are writing this letter to help those who come after you. Will this help you? Only indirectly. This is part of your actions to take control of your own life.

Maintain pride in yourself!
This is extremely important. You are the most important person in your world. Be kind to yourself. If you have made mistakes, learn from them. We all make mistakes. Mistakes do *not* make you less of a person. It is the inability to learn from one's mistakes that limits one's growth. Negative experiences occur in the lives of all persons who push their limits. It is up to you to convert this negative experience into a positive experience, and the easiest way to do this is to learn and grow as a result of the experience.

Explore your possible options and land on your feet!
Having learned and grown as a result of this negative experience, now decide on your future options. Seldom does a door close without the opening of at least one other door. Throughout life, as we discuss in section **XX**, the intelligent person always plans ahead. Yes, you have focused most of your attention and energies on completion of the graduate program, but in the background, you have been considering the alternative plans.

120

Explore your special set of skills:
You have a special set of skills that got you into graduate school in the first place. You've learned in graduate school, and you have learned as a result of your experiences in leaving graduate school. In other words, you are now even more qualified than before. The only thing you need is the opportunity to demonstrate those qualifications. Don't dwell on the negative experience. Life is ahead of you. Take your lessons and go for it.

XX

Leaving Graduate School

It may seem to the student in graduate school that their graduate program will extend forever. However, the reality is that you *will* leave graduate school. This leaving may be after completion of your graduate program with degree in hand; this leaving may be without degree sometime in the middle of your graduate program as a consequence of a decision to pursue a different path; or this leaving may be the consequence of a decision by the graduate school, your research advisor, *etc.* that you *must* leave the graduate program. In any of these circumstances, your graduate program *will* come to an end. In this section, we will cover some of the steps that you should take *during* your graduate program to smooth the path following your graduate program. You only need two pieces of advice: plan ahead, and keep good records.

Plan ahead!

In your graduate program, you are developing at least two major attributes: maturity and the capacity for analytical, scholarly thought. One characteristic of the mature person with the capacity for analytical, scholarly thought is his/her ability to constantly plan ahead. This is not meant merely as planning the next step, but rather as planning a network beyond the present. Thus, as an example, one might think: "if this idea proves to be correct, then the following steps will be taken; if, on the other hand, this idea proves not to be correct, then the following alternative steps will be taken."

One characteristic of many undergraduate students is that the future plans go through the week, possibly to the next test, and rarely through the next year. You wish to develop the ability to plan far beyond the present.

Based upon your present collection of information, where do you want to be in ten years? What are the necessary steps to get there? At each of these steps, what is the alternative plan? Plan beyond the graduate degree and have alternatives in place. The more thorough your plan, the less you will be perturbed by random events around you. In addition, with thorough planning, if you find that your goals were based on inadequate information, your entire life need not be thrown into disarray. If you find that the pursuit of a graduate degree is not an appropriate step, you will smoothly alter your journey without feeling that you have failed.

Note well that your choice of mentors (Chapter **IX**) depends in great part on the skills that you will need in the future. In order to intelligently choose these mentors, you must have a plan for your future. For example, do you wish ultimately to be an educator? If so, you need a mentor who can guide you toward acquiring the skills of an educator. There are many career opportunities for those with graduate degrees, so be sure to explore as many options as possible early enough in your graduate program to develop the needed skills. Possibly the worst thing you could do is to plan based on the goal of being your mentor's clone.

Keep good records!
As you are completing your advanced degree, you will be applying for positions. As part of your application, you will include a *curriculum vitae* or *C.V.*, which is a professional biography. In this *C.V.*, you will include all of the steps of your professional life, such as positions held, degrees, professional presentations, courses taught, *etc.* Request that your research advisor show you what a *curriculum vitae* for your field looks like, and begin to develop this document during your first year. At the end of *each* term, update the *curriculum vitae.* When you are preparing to apply for positions, this important component of your application will be ready. The form of the C.V. will vary by field, so use the example from your research advisor, not from a generic on-line sample.

For additional readings, see the following:

Bolker, J. 1998. *Writing your dissertation in fifteen minutes a day: a guide to starting, revising and finishing your doctoral thesis.* Owl Books.

Gosling, P. A. & B. D. Noordam. 2006. *Mastering your Ph.D.: survival and success in the doctoral years and beyond.* Springer.

Mumbe, D. G. 2004. *Graduate school: winning strategies for getting in with or without excellent grades.* Proto Press.

Peters, R. L. 1997. *Getting what you came for: The smart student's guide to earning a master's or a Ph.D.* Noonday Press.

Phillips, E. M. & D. S. Pugh. 2010. *How to get a PhD.: a handbook for students and their supervisors.* 4th Ed. Open University Press.

The Ziibi Press is the publishing arm of the Center for the Study of Indigenous Border Issues (CSIBI) which is incorporated in the State of Michigan as an educational non-profit organization. (Ziibi is the Ojibwe word for "river" --as in Mississippi).

While the main focus of CSIBI is concerned with the *political boundaries* that often divide Indigenous Peoples, the concept of "border issues" for us is much broader.

Other boundaries that Indigenous people must often transverse are those that separate our cultures from that of the visitors. That is, we wish to explore what it means to be an Indigenous person in this era of mass consumption and environmental destruction.

This book is our first publishing effort and it explores that "border" between Indigenous communities and "The Academy" –especially, graduate school. Many disadvantaged students fail to negotiate that "higher-ed" boundary. We are hopeful that the information in this book will help reverse that trend.

CSIBI Directors:
Phil Bellfy, Michigan State University, East Lansing
Karl Hele, Concordia University, Montreal
David McNab, York University, Toronto
Please visit our website for more information: <http://csibi.org/>